# WHY WOMEN KILL

# WHY WOMEN KILL

## HOMICIDE AND GENDER EQUALITY

VICKIE JENSEN

LYNNE
RIENNER
PUBLISHERS

BOULDER
LONDON

Published in the United States of America in 2001 by
Lynne Rienner Publishers, Inc.
1800 30th Street, Boulder, Colorado 80301
www.rienner.com

and in the United Kingdom by
Lynne Rienner Publishers, Inc.
3 Henrietta Street, Covent Garden, London WC2E 8LU

**Library of Congress Cataloging-in-Publication Data**
Jensen, Vickie, 1967–
    Why women kill : homicide and gender equality / Vickie Jensen.
        p.   cm.
    Includes bibliographical references and index.
    ISBN 1-58826-027-5 (alk. paper)
    1. Women murderers.   2. Family violence.   3. Women's rights.   I. Title.
HV6517.J46   2001
364.15'23'—dc21

                                                                    2001031962

**British Cataloguing in Publication Data**
A Cataloguing in Publication record for this book
is available from the British Library.

Printed and bound in the United States of America

        The paper used in this publication meets the requirements
  ∞     of the American National Standard for Permanence of
        Paper for Printed Library Materials Z39.48-1984.

    5   4   3   2   1

# CONTENTS

# ACKNOWLEDGMENTS

This book is a product of nearly eight years of work that started with an exploration of gender and homicide. There are several people along the way who have been instrumental in both helping with the development of the content of the book and in the personal encouragement and support of its author. First, I must thank Bridget Julian and Shena Redmond of Lynne Rienner Publishers. It was Bridget who saw potential in the project and went above and beyond her duties as acquisitions editor to help me get this published. She worked with me on the development of the manuscript and offered solid advice during the revision process; without Bridget there truly would have been no book. Shena did a marvelous job of taking the approved manuscript and turning it into this final product. Their work, advice, and patience will always be appreciated.

There have been several colleagues and advisers who have provided invaluable moral support and academic assistance. Members of my dissertation committee at the University of Colorado—Kirk Williams, Del Elliott, Fred Pampel, Gary Marx, and David Huizinga—need to be thanked not only for reading and approving my ideas and analysis but for challenging me to make them better. I do not believe that I could have assembled a better group of scholars to help me develop the core of this work. I also received excellent technical support from colleagues at the University of Colorado. Jani Little provided expert assistance with statistical analysis. I must also acknowledge Brian Mattson and the Center for the Study and Prevention of Violence for providing data and clerical support during that time.

While writing, I received encouragement from all of my sociology colleagues at California State University, Northridge, who were happy to offer their expertise and moral support. I must especially thank Jane Prather, who read the entire manuscript and gave feedback that enhanced my discussion of the gender issues included here. I also need to thank my students for their insights. The Research and Sponsored Projects office at the university provided me with a semester of reassigned time, which gave me the opportunity to begin revisions. I also must thank two anonymous readers who reviewed the work and offered valuable suggestions.

I would be remiss to forget friends and family who have listened to me patiently and provided me refuge when I was stressed out and needed comfort. I cannot list you all, but you all made significant contributions. Karren, Elizabeth, Dan, Ronnie, and Alan have been especially wonderful. My parents have always been there, encouraging me and anxiously awaiting the final product, even when they were not sure exactly what I was doing. I must thank my husband, Chris, who has at various times been a comforting friend, cheerleader, intellectual sounding board, computer technician, typist, and my first editor. It is difficult to find someone who can wear so many hats, and I feel fortunate to have him around to wear them all.

I must also recognize a group that has personally introduced me to the topic of women who kill: the women of Mabel Bassett Correctional Center. These women were the ones who first taught me what it means to be an oppressed woman and how lethal violence can come from any woman from any walk of life. Unfortunately, that reality was once again underscored by the arrest of my friend Cynthia. I hope that society can reach the goal of no woman being abused, when no woman is left to feel that killing her abusive partner is the only way out. This book is dedicated to the quest to achieve these ends.

—*Vickie Jensen*

# 1

# Introduction: Women, Gender, and Homicide

When we hear the word *killer,* who usually comes to mind? We imagine dark figures lurking in alleys, awaiting new victims, and brutal robbers who assassinate store clerks after looting cash drawers. When women are identified as homicide suspects or seen being arrested, we are shocked. Regardless of whether the victims are family members, acquaintances, or strangers, women who kill present a sharp contrast to the common image society holds of the homicide offender as tough, scary, and male.

Women do commit homicide. Although they do so at a lesser rate than men, women's homicide is an important component of society's experience with lethal violence. Federal Bureau of Investigation (FBI) statistics show that those who commit homicide are predominantly, but not exclusively, male. According to FBI Uniform Crime Reports statistics (FBI, 1996), 1,384 (10.3 percent) of the 13,466 people arrested for murder and nonnegligent manslaughter that year were women. Even though women are the minority of homicide offenders, women do kill.

Several compelling reasons exist to examine a group that constitutes such a small percentage of offenders. First and obviously, we should look at women who kill because of the seriousness of the crime and its repercussions; we should also examine victim impact. For every woman homicide offender, there is at least one victim. Thus over 1,000 persons every year are killed by women. In addition to those whose lives are cut short, many loved ones must grieve and cope with the loss of the victims.

The seriousness of women's homicide is also seen in its effects on those in the offenders' lives. Homicide's serious penalties take women offenders from their children and other family members, who are negatively affected by the sudden absence. Loved ones must cope with the offender being sent to prison, often for life. This is particularly difficult for children, some of whom may have lost both father and mother within a very short period. Society suffers as well when the children of incarcerated mothers end up on public assistance through foster care or financially burdened relatives.

Studying women who kill is also important because it gives us insight into the quality of women's lives. This becomes more clear when we directly examine the situations in which women kill. Women's homicide victims are found disproportionately in the traditional, domestic sphere: they are often intimate partners and family members (see, for example, Browne, Williams, and Dutton, 1999; Websdale, 1999; Browne, 1987; Totman, 1978; Browne and Williams, 1989, 1993; Wilbanks, 1983). These homicides often occur in the context of domestic abuse or other intense conflict and when no other solution to a desperate situation can be seen. For example, Angela Browne and Kirk Williams (1989) found that a lack of resources available to women who need to leave situations in which they are battered by intimate partners increases the rate at which women kill.

The gendered nature of women's lives has an important influence on their tendency to commit homicide. Being a woman, particularly in some situations, can influence the context of a killing. Prior to committing homicide, women most often face situations that directly relate to their location within a gender-stratified society. Homicide by women is often directly linked to domestic violence, desperation and fear around parenting, and involvement with men who are criminals. Thus women are more likely to commit homicide when they are victimized, trapped by traditional expectations, and denied adequate resources to escape bad domestic situations that lead to desperation and inescapable and unbearable life situations. These are clear indicators that women are experiencing a low quality of life, and homicide represents its most serious extreme. Indeed, women's homicide offending can be seen as the outcome of one extreme end of a continuum reflecting women's quality of life and well-being. At the other end, women would be free from domestic abuse, valued in public and private life, and free to express their complete humanity.

## Defining Gender Equality

The research on women who kill comes back to the forces that affect the way women live their lives and the fact that homicide often reflects the inequalities and disadvantages women have faced by virtue of being women. In this book the term *gender equality* is used as a representation of these forces. Gender equality, then, becomes a lens through which we can view women who kill. Gender equality has historically had many meanings and emphases, some of which conflict with each other. Thus I define gender equality for my purposes here.

Gender equality, most broadly, refers to ideal structural and cultural conditions, with parity for women and men. Scholars have described women's positions in less than equal conditions as disadvantaged with regard to power, privilege, and opportunity—all of which are distributed differentially in ways that benefit men more than women. Gender stratification has also been used to describe ways in which men and women inhabit different and unequal places in society, with men in general occupying the higher strata with regard to valued resources. Janet Chafetz (1991) defined gender stratification–gender equality in this way: "The degree of gender stratification in a society refers to the extent to which females are systematically disadvantaged to these values [resources] relative to males in their own society who are otherwise their social equals" (76). Dana Dunn and colleagues (1993) also described these differences in terms of access to valued resources and opportunities differentially distributed between men and women.

Drawing from this initial discussion, I use the term *gender equality* to refer to the state in which men and women have equal access to valued resources. In a state of gender equality, the gender of otherwise equal persons will have no impact on their life chances, opportunities, expectations, or other features of their social lives. Gender equality is conceptualized as a variable representing degrees of the gender equality ideal whose levels are worthy of study as predictors of behavior.[1] Thus I will refer to gender equality achievement in discussing its influence on homicide and other behaviors. I acknowledge that not all places or times will necessarily have the same levels of equality (see also Sugarman and Straus, 1988; Yllo, 1983).

These inequalities can be broadly conceptualized in three categories: economic, political-legal, and social. These general categorizations were derived from two sources. First, with the exception of social equality, David Sugarman and Murray Straus (1988) used these divisions in the creation of their state-level measure of gender equality. Second, these are the most common themes in the research on gender. The addition of social equality comes directly from such thematic categorizing and from the observation that it has not been included in other quantitative gender equality indexes.[2]

## Economic Equality

One dimension of gender equality is economic. Researchers have identified inequities in economic opportunities, wages, occupational prestige, patterns of inheritance, and other areas related to economics and the labor force (e.g., Williams, 1995; Abbott and Wallace, 1990; Chafetz, 1991). These inequities relate to women's ability to participate equally in the world of work and to receive compensation for that work equal to that of men in the same positions. Work done by men is usually more valued, is better paid, and is rewarded with more upward mobility, responsibility, and prestige than women's work—even when men work in "women's" professions (Williams, 1995). Such economic inequalities can lead to further economic marginalization, poverty, and dependency of women, particularly when they are caring for children.

A related issue is education. Women have reached the same level of high school completion as men but still trail men in the number of undergraduate and advanced degrees. Many women still have not acquired the education and job training required to make a decent wage. According to Kathleen Ferraro (1997), job training is one of the most important needs of battered women who leave relationships. Traditionally, women have been disadvantaged in terms of both educational attainment and the quality of training for highly skilled, high-paid jobs.

## Political and Legal Equality

Women have not achieved equal representation in the political arena. Government decisions are made by executives, legislators, and other groups that are still predominantly male (Mossman, 1994; MacKinnon, 1987). As Catharine MacKinnon (1987) argues, however, representation is not enough; for the political sphere to be equal, women's voices have to count as much as men's in all levels of decisionmaking. The basis for real political power has changed little, even with increasing representation of women in local, state, and federal government.

In addition to equality in politics is the degree to which the genders are equal with respect to the legal and criminal justice system. The lack of power women hold in government bodies can result in laws and policies that do not reflect women's interests, positions, needs, or perspectives. Women have also not received fair treatment by and under the law.[3] MacKinnon (1987) argues that the law is not fair as long as it is based on a hierarchical system dominated by male standards and that women are disadvantaged in such a system, either through a lack of protection or through "equal opportunity" laws that deny critical differences and hinder women in ways specific to their being women.

Women are also unequal under the law as applied to women lawbreakers. For example, Christy Visher (1983) found that the likelihood of a woman's arrest is greatly shaped by the degree to which she adheres to women's traditional norms of passivity and compliance. Meda Chesney-Lind (1989, 1992 with Shelden) demonstrated that gender stereotypes and girls' appearance strongly influence juvenile justice detainment and court processing. Both Cynthia Gillespie (1989) and Ferraro (1997) described a judicial system that often does not take women's battering into account in the cases of such women who kill. Some formal changes have been made to alter evidentiary standards to admit battered women's syndrome and other testimony regarding abuse, but in other ways—many of them informal—experiences of abuse are not taken into account during pretrial hearings and activities, actual trials, and sentencing.

Correctional institutions for women are often insensitive to some of women's special needs (e.g., pre- and post-childbirth needs, children's issues, and abuse issues) and usually offer gender-stereotypical programs that reinforce traditional roles and low-paying positions

in society. Programs that build skills for higher-paying, more financially independent careers are offered less frequently at women's
institutions than at men's. As a confounding feature of the criminal
justice system, women are disproportionately represented as workers
in police forces, the judiciary, and corrections, particularly with
regard to positions of authority (Belknap, 1996). Gender equality in
politics and the law would include equal representation and voice for
women in the making of law, fair treatment by and protection under
the legal and criminal justice systems, and equal representation of
women in all levels of the criminal justice system—both in total
numbers and in positions of power and authority. In light of the lack
of achievement of this ideal, we must look at the degree it is present
to measure its effects on other social phenomena, including homicide.

## Social Equality

Social equality, for the purposes of this book, is defined as the state
in which normative expectations, in content and degree, are applied
equally to men and women. It also includes equality in culture where
the value of cultural contributions, symbols, meanings, and other
products and of persons themselves is equal regardless of gender.
Social equality carries the equal opportunity for both genders to play
a full range of social roles in families, relationships, the workplace,
social gatherings, and other social groupings. Conceptually, the concept of social equality extends throughout social interaction and
expected roles and behaviors.

Several authors have noted key components of these social
equality structures in terms of gender, regardless of whether the term
*social equality* was used. The ideological value and symbolism of the
family and its domestic roles for women were discussed by Joan
Chandler (1991), who argued that society restricts opportunities for
and undervalues women who are not living with husbands. Miriam
Johnson (1988) argued that traditional, legal marriage is inherently
unequal because of the gendered division of roles and expectations.
Women's roles are clearly in the home and with children, whereas
men's roles include work outside the home for financial provision, as
well as the role of family leader. These roles are part of the legal
structure of the marriage contract and of the social constructs of married persons.

The concept of gender role equality is seen in discussions of difference between genders. Many writers describe a polarity in the divisions between men and women, characterized by low or no overlap of acceptable behaviors. This polarity is seen in definitions of self, identity, and appropriate behavior for self and others by gender. Polarity between genders is characterized by rigid distinctions between expectations and the relative value given men and women (see Stoltenburg, 1999; Wolf, 1999; Messerschmidt, 1993, 1995; Connell, 1995). Simone de Beauvoir (1953) described these distinctions as creating complete separation between the genders. She argued that relations between men and women are the binary oppositions of Subject and Object, which, by definition, are mutually exclusive categories. Men, as Subject, are the central reference point, the standard against which all others are measured. Object includes those who are devalued, acted upon, and controlled by the Subject, including women and "not-men." "Not-men" includes those men who violate the standards of "man" and thus are not viewed as real men, which relegates them to the same devalued status women occupy as Object. Objects' control over their own and others' lives, rewards, and expectations is minimal, if it exists at all.

These distinctions result in social gender polarities in which masculinity is defined in opposition to femininity. Hegemonic masculinity—the ideal cultural expectations of strength, domination, work, and the like—exerts a strong influence on men to enact masculinity as a way of being properly defined as a "man." To be a man means to not be a woman, and femininity separate from actual women becomes a negative pole against which men are defined (see, for example, Kimmel, 1996; Connell, 1995). The opposite of men's expected and valued action constitutes the definition and expectations of women: weak, submissive, emotionally driven, and tending to domestic, unpaid duties (Connell, 1995; Messerschmidt, 1993, 1995; Levant and Kopecky, 1995; Morgan, 1992; Messner and Rosenfeld, 1999).

The stronger the focus on these gender-divisive distinctions, the weaker the acceptance of crossover role behaviors. Women should not "act like men," and the only good man is a "real man." This limits the full expression of the social self for men and women. The difference is that men still retain the power that comes from the norms and expectations that make them men, and they maintain the power to make those definitions.

Gender equality is an ideal not met anywhere in contemporary Western society. Thus the degree to which gender equality exists is an important measurement of women's and men's relative positions in the gender system. Quantification, as is done in this analysis, of the influences of gender equality requires that it be seen in this way. The discussion here has limitations, as it is driven in part toward quantifiable concepts and summary categorizations. However limited the definitions of gender equality in this book, it is clear in the research that gender is one of the biggest influences on the way we live our lives. As such, it is critical to our understanding of many social phenomena, including homicide.

## Gender Equality and Women's Homicide

Gender equality provides one of the strongest theoretical and empirical explanations addressing women who commit homicide, particularly domestic homicide. It also provides the most promising direction for policies to improve women's lives and, as such, to decrease the risk that women will commit lethal violence.[4] It has received little attention in homicide research. The few studies that have included gender equality measures in analyses of women's homicide offending rates have found that gender equality significantly decreases the rate at which women kill (Best and Luckinbill, 1990; Weisheit, 1993). This suggests that the structural features of gender have an important impact on the lives of women, and women's opportunity and equality result in lower rates of women's homicide. Women primarily kill intimate partners and family, so the connection between women's overall homicide offending rates and gender equality lies largely in the connection between gender stratification and women's domestic lives. These findings suggest that a promising approach to decreasing women's homicide offending is to increase gender equality.

The goal of this book is to investigate the connections among gender equality and opportunity, women's lives, and homicide offending. The book considers the theoretical and empirical basis for using gendered explanations of women's lethal violence. These gender-homicide connections are presented theoretically, and they are presented empirically using official FBI homicide data from 1990 that detail homicides, broken down by gender, for cities with populations over 100,000.[5] Both in theory and with data, therefore, this study demonstrates the importance of gender structures when trying to explain why women kill. The intersections of race, class, and age in the gender-homicide connection are important to a complete examination of women who kill. Although this book explores the influence of gender equality on women's homicide offending, it does not incorporate race, class, and age in its analysis. This exclusion should not be interpreted as a denial of the importance of diversity in understanding women who kill. Rather, it results from a paucity of data and theory development sufficient to move beyond a superficial discussion that may reify rather than examine stereotypical conclusions. This work instead addresses the common and general effects of gender structures in women's homicide.

## Patterns of Homicide by Gender

One of the most important indicators that gender needs further investigation is the striking difference in men's and women's homicide offending patterns. The victim-offender relationship is an important consideration. The killing of intimate partners, children, and other family members reflects a homicidal context involving very close relationships—a context that may not be directly influenced by public interaction or discourse. Instead, domestic conflicts are most common in the private sphere, whereas the killing of acquaintances and strangers largely occurs in the public sphere involving persons who do not know each other intimately or do not know each other at all prior to the homicidal event. This kind of lethal violence also includes a much greater proportion of felony-related crimes such as homicides committed during robberies.

Patterns of victim-offender relationships differ greatly between men and women. Proportionally, women kill family members and intimate partners more often than men, although the total in all victim-offender categories is higher for men than for women (see, for example, Holmes and Holmes, 1994). In William Wilbanks's (1983) examination of 1980 FBI Supplementary Homicide Report data, women killed family members 14.5 percent of the time and lovers or spouses 45.1 percent of the time; thus 59.6 percent of women's victims were intimate or domestic. In the research reported in this book, the percentage of family and intimate partner victims in murders by women in cities over 100,000 was a very similar 57.4 percent. Thus women's victims are largely persons involved in domestic interaction. Other researchers have also found that family and intimate partners constitute the highest percentage of women's homicide victims (Browne, Williams, and Dutton, 1999; Websdale, 1999; Goetting, 1988; Jurik and Gregware, 1992; Mann, 1988, 1992, 1996; Jurik and Winn, 1990; Silverman and Kennedy, 1988). Strangers, on the other hand, are the rarest among women's victims. In Wilbanks's (1983) data they constituted only 6.7 percent of victims; in the 1990 data analyzed here, strangers comprised just 6.9 percent of women's victims.

Compared with women, men are much more likely to kill acquaintances and strangers and much less likely to kill family members and lovers or spouses. In 1980 Supplementary Homicide Report data, Wilbanks reports that family members or lovers/spouses were the distinct minority of men's homicide victims (Wilbanks, 1983). In the 1990 data analyzed here, intimates accounted for 16.8 percent of men's homicide victims, 30.7 percent were strangers, and 52.5 percent were acquaintances. Men, when they kill, are *least* likely to kill intimates, whereas women are *most* likely to kill intimates. This difference points strongly to the potential effects of social life in the public sphere, traditionally occupied by men, and the domestic sphere, traditionally occupied by women. As gender impacts interaction in these spheres, gender must also impact the context of homicides by men and women.

The patterns of homicide by men and women also differ when we examine the circumstances under which homicide is committed. Men's homicide offending is much more likely than that of women to include economic motives or to occur while committing another felony (Wilbanks, 1983). Women rarely commit homicide for economic gain or while committing felonies (Jurik and Winn, 1990; Mann, 1992). When women commit homicide for economic reasons, their involvement is usually secondary. Nancy Jurik and Peter Gregware (1992) found that when economic gain was a motive for women, they were usually accessories.

The reasons women commit homicide mostly involve interpersonal conflict and self-defense in a response to abuse and direct attack. Fights, arguments, and abuse are often primary reasons women commit homicide (Silverman, Vega, and Danner, 1993; Ward, Jackson, and Ward, 1979). Such conflicts and responses to violence include domestic arguments, confrontation, abuse, and defense of self or others (Goetting, 1988; Jurik and Gregware, 1992; Jurik and Winn, 1990). Several women's homicides in these studies involved prior conflicts and aggression. In examining women's homicide cases in Phoenix, Jurik and Russ Winn (1990) found that prior conflicts existed in 60 percent of cases and that 44 percent involved physical aggression. When women who acted alone were examined separately, 73 percent of homicides involved prior conflicts, 55 percent with physical aggression. In only those cases involving intimate partners, 86 percent involved physical conflict.

Many homicidal contexts involving women have directly included self-defense or victim precipitation. *Victim precipitation* is a term used to refer to a situation in which the victim contributed to his or her death, usually through direct attack, provocation, or other instigation by the offender. Victim precipitation and self-defense are used in the literature to reflect circumstances in which the victim helped to create the situation of his or her own death. Self-defense or victim precipitation is present especially in cases of intimate partner homicide (e.g., Browne, Williams, and Dutton, 1999; Browne, 1987, 1997; Websdale, 1999; Langan and Dawson, 1995). The precipitating event to a woman's homicide is often a physical attack against her or another reason to fear for her life or well-being. A large number of cases in which women are offenders involve victim provocation and self-defense, and those figures are higher than those in homicide cases in general (Goetting, 1988; Jurik and Gregware, 1992; Mann, 1988, 1992; Cazenave and Zahn, 1992; Langan and Dawson, 1995). In contrast, a much smaller number of cases in which women kill involve premeditation; that is, their homicides are usually not planned in advance. Jurik and Winn (1990) found that 27 percent of their cases had preplanned the homicide, and Coramae Mann (1992) found that 29.9 percent of the cases she examined were preplanned.

## Intimate Partner Homicide

Intimate partners are women's most frequent homicide victims. A strong connection is found between women's victimization by intimate partners and the incidence of homicide women commit against those partners. Such homicides are often the end result of physical, sexual, and emotional abuse that has escalated to the point that women feel their well-being and even their lives are in immediate danger, and they kill as an effort toward self-preservation or in self-defense.

Women stay in such dangerous relationships for many reasons, many of which are directly related to gender structures. First, traditional social expectations can play a role in supporting violent marriages. Traditional norms include an emphasis on legal marriage, the reinforcement of women's responsibility to keep men happy, discouragement of women's efforts to leave unhappy—even violent—marriages, and the expectation that men will control and exert dominance over the household. Traditional marriage is a legal contract that is difficult to end—particularly when considering child custody, alimony or other support, the division of assets, and so forth—and women may see these complications as a deterrent to leaving abusive situations.

Socially, women may stay in bad marriages and abusive situations as they respond to the expectation that women are responsible for the needs of the children and men in their lives. When women are taught to believe it is their job to keep the family happy, leaving a marriage is an admission of failure and is unlikely to receive social support.

An additional influence of an unequal gender system is the power men have to control the family; they often receive support for the use of domination, including physical abuse, to maintain that control. The stronger the emphasis on women's role in making men happy, keeping the household together, and being submissive, the stronger the power of men to be primary providers, to expect that the home will be managed properly, and to maintain and enforce dominance. Men's violence against women is thus more legitimized and more likely to occur.

The gender conditions that keep women in abusive relationships and that simultaneously support men's control and use of violence to maintain their power increase the likelihood that women will kill their intimate partners. In both the work of Browne and Williams (1989) and the analysis presented here, strong support is seen for the argument that men's violence against intimate partners increases women's intimate partner homicide offending. Men's violence against women and women's killing of intimate partners are thus intricately connected.

Gender equality and inequality is another crucial deterrent to women's attempts to leave violent home situations. Gender inequality limits the economic and social support opportunities to help women leave abusive relationships and live independently. The lower the level of gender equality, the less likely it is that critical assistance such as employment, decent wages, and supports such as shelters will exist to help battered women. For example, the availability of battered women's shelters in Browne and Williams's (1989) study and the rate of women's employment in the present study significantly reduced women's rates of intimate partner killing, adding supportive evidence for the critical role such resources play. Clearly, gender equality can positively impact women's lives and decrease homicide offending by providing economic and social support structures.

In general, we find support for the contention that women's intimate partner homicide rates decrease with increased gender equality. Such equality can decrease the emphasis and value given to men's violence against women and decrease the likelihood that women will need to use self-defensive action against abusive men. Additionally, gender equality can place the necessary emphasis on improving the resources women need to escape such situations prior to a lethal escalation of violence.

## Family Homicide

Cases in which women kill family members also show the connection between structural gender conditions that affect women's lives and the context in which they kill. Women who kill family members other than intimate partners are often in situations of economic and social entrapment that contribute to them killing infants, children, and elders—the largest proportion of family victims. These economic and social forces, similar to those in intimate partner homicide, are directly linked both theoretically and empirically to the degree of equality and opportunity in their status as women.

The link between gender equality and opportunities and the rates of women's family homicide is rooted in three primary areas: (1) social norms that differentially emphasize women's nurturing and responsibility for caring for family members, (2) an economic opportunity structure that disadvantages women in terms of salary and work opportunities while caring for family members, and (3) a lack of government attention to the financial and program needs of women who are caring for dependent children and elderly family members. Such disadvantages can increase the likelihood that women will abuse children and elders and can also increase other kinds of entrapment that could make a vulnerable family member the target of a woman's anger and frustration.[6] These factors increase the risk of homicide committed as either abuse gone too far or a last desperate act of a woman who could see no other way out.

Elements of social gender inequalities are often at play in the development of homicidal events involving family members. In addition to being unpaid, women's work is often given little social value. This is particularly true for women's unpaid caregiving, which often involves sole or disproportionate responsibility for a dependent person. If low gender equality exists, this work is expected of women and not of men and results in competing demands for time and energy. Traditionally, women have been expected to do this work without complaint and without emotional and social support such as child care or shared responsibilities. These conditions often result in extreme stress and frustration (Fox and Allen, 1987; Klein, 1995; Hooyman and Ryan, 1987).

Economic inequalities further disadvantage women caregivers. Women's disproportionate representation in low-paying, low-status jobs in general, supported by traditional beliefs about women's low level of commitment to work and careers, results in fewer financial resources. Women who are supporting children and others in the home are disadvantaged by inequities in financial compensation and promotions and in flexible scheduling. Financial resources can assist with caregiving burdens, but women caregivers are the least likely to have access to those resources. Such economic difficulties further intensify the stress women may feel when caring for dependent family members. When economic resources *are* available, the negative impact of familial stress is more likely to be mitigated (National Research Council, 1993; Milner and Crouch, 1993).

The labor market and wages provide little help for women involved in caregiving, and they are also unlikely to receive assistance from official sources. Financial support of caregivers is not a priority of government programs, as is readily seen in the lack of a comprehensive, national child care support system. The lack of child care subsidies puts many economically disadvantaged women in a proverbial corner in which paying for child care may be a burdensome expense out of paychecks that are already too small.

Gender-family homicide connections are found in the abuse and homicide literature, which shows a strong connection between inadequate economic resources and child abuse (National Research Council, 1993; Milner and Crouch, 1993; Gelles, 1993). The same connection has been seen in studies of elder abuse (Finkelhor and Pillemer, 1988; Hooyman and Ryan, 1987). Research on homicide committed by women against children has revealed economic deprivation, financial strain, and other economic losses (Totman, 1978; Ogle, Maier-Katkin, and Bernard, 1995; Holmes and Holmes, 1994; Weisheit, 1986; Mann, 1993; Websdale, 1999). Social spending by government agencies has been shown to decrease the rates of child homicide in general (Messner and Rosenfeld, 1999). My research found that men's greater sharing of parenting chores decreased the likelihood that women would kill family members. Combined with less visible but very real social norms, such conditions combine to create an environment in which homicide against a family member may occur.

A close link also exists among gender conditions, stress, and other violence against family members in such situations. Stress has been defined as a major trigger in child abuse (Milner and Crouch, 1993; Gelles, 1993), elder abuse (Boudreau, 1993; Hooyman and Ryan, 1987), and the killing of children (Holmes and Holmes, 1994; Totman, 1978; Weisheit, 1986; Silverman and Kennedy, 1988). In the context of some of the social and economic limitations discussed earlier, stress can result in feelings of entrapment (Totman, 1978; Websdale, 1999). When one feels trapped and options appear (and often are) limited, lethal violence is more likely to occur. As N. Prabha Unnithan and colleagues (1994) present, stress can become objectified and externalized so that the source of the stress is identified as the person who is dependent. This is the kind of process that leads to homicide. These observations are supported by Jane Totman's (1978) finding that women who kill children see their children as irritating and symbolic of their frustrations and failures. These actions are more likely to occur when women lack the social freedom to seek assistance for caregiving deemed to be the domain of women and also lack the economic resources to provide relief from what is a stressful and often frustrating job—caring for dependents.

In brief, gender equality is applicable in thinking about women who kill family members as well as intimate partners. The nature of gender equality and family homicide connections is discussed more fully in theory in Chapter 2 and empirically in Chapter 4.

## Differences in Theory Application by Gender

In criminology and in sociology in general, many theories are not examined to see if they apply equally well to men and women. Describing it as the "generalizability problem" in criminology, Kathleen Daly and Meda Chesney-Lind (1988) call for criminologists to examine their theories to see if they explain women's homicide offending as well as they do men's. Few studies have examined theory in this way, though. Darrell Steffensmeier and Dana Haynie (2000) are an exception. In a brief discussion of homicide, they find that structural predictors derived from traditional theories were less predictive of women's likelihood to commit homicide than of men's. They point to women's disproportionate numbers of infant and partner killings as an explanation but do not more fully consider the theoretical implications.

By failing to examine fully homicide with women's and men's data separated, criminology has presumed that the same theories work equally well by gender. When no such comparison is done, research also assumes that men and women respond similarly to the factors that increase homicide. Theoretically, these issues have not been explored either. Assuming sameness denies differences in men's and women's lives, opportunities, and social expectations. In short, assuming generalizability works only in a society that is not stratified by gender and, in terms used here, is gender equal. In addition to the weaknesses of a "gender-blind" approach to theory with regard to women's homicide, the underlying assumptions of sameness do not hold up in the face of empirical data.

This book examines these "equal effect" presumptions both theoretically and empirically. It first theoretically critiques the three dominant perspectives (social disorganization–community disruption, economic deprivation, and cultural-subcultural) in homicide study. This book also analyzes these theory-derived predictors using women-only and men-only homicide rates to test whether men and women are equally affected by the factors they outline. Chapter 2 critiques the potential weaknesses and incorrect assumptions of the most important "general" homicide theories using gender, and Chapter 4 empirically examines variables commonly drawn from those theories.

Empirical evidence supports the contention that these theoretical models do not explain women's and men's homicide equally well. From analysis reported here, women's homicide is less explainable using gender-blind theoretical indicators. This finding demonstrates that men's and women's homicide offending patterns are not the same and that ignoring the influences of these variables on women's lives in the development of homicide theories makes those theories best suited to predict lethal violence committed by men.

One exception to this conclusion may be homicide involving intimate partners. Men's rates of such homicide are even more poorly explained by traditional variables than women's, although several indicators are statistically significant. As this kind of homicide has a *domestic* context, the most important divisions in homicide may be those between private and public spheres. We see women most often in the domestic sphere, so the traditional theories appear better suited to men's homicide (a point also made by Steffensmeier and Haynie, 2000). Men's homicides tend to occur in the public sphere, and public homicide may be best explained with these structural variables. Therefore we might argue that gender is less significant than context.

Closer inspection of the data reveals that similarities are found because men's and women's intimate partner homicide results largely from the same kinds of contextual dynamics, characterized most strongly by the abuse of women in relationships. Theoretically, we can see different reasons for homicides committed by women versus those of men. If men are the abusers, as is primarily the case, killing their partners is the extreme and ultimate end of a long cycle of violence. For women, it is a desperate act to end the violence before it kills them. In both cases the structural factors are likely working through the men's violence rather than through women's homicidal acts. Additional empirical analysis reveals that men's violence against women, measured by men's intimate partner homicide rates, contributes strongly and significantly to women's likelihood to kill intimate partners, thereby accounting for many of the observed similarities. Thus even though the results by gender are similar at this point, women's experiences and disadvantages regarding life in the home are critical for understanding why they kill intimate partners.

By examining the victim-offender context, circumstances in which men and women kill, and differences in applications of traditional homicide theory, we begin to see some observable and important differences between the two genders. Women are more likely than men to kill family members and intimate partners, and they most often do so in response to conflict, abuse, and direct attack from the victim that makes lethal violence more likely. For men, a majority of victims are acquaintances or strangers, and their homicides are more frequently related to felonies and economic gain. The fact that women are women makes a difference in their likelihood to commit homicide. Furthermore, the importance of the domestic sphere women inhabit warrants further discussion. Current homicide theory cannot explain women's homicides as well as men's largely because gender differences are not considered.

## Analyzing Women's Homicide: Empirical Support for Gender Equality Measures

Women's homicides are tightly connected to women's lives and the disadvantages entailed in low gender equality. Theoretically, links exist between gender structures and women's homicide offending. Empirical support also supports the conclusion that gender equality is important in understanding women who kill. Relatively few studies directly address gender equality and women's homicide offending other than what is presented here. Three that do are Joel Best and David Luckinbill (1990), Browne and Williams (1989), and Ralph Weisheit (1993). Their results reveal the necessity for further empirical examination of the ways in which gender equality and women's homicide offending are connected.

These studies demonstrate that levels of gender equality and opportunity have an important influence on women's likelihood to commit homicide. Using state-level indexes of gender equality, Best and Luckinbill (1990) and Weisheit (1993) found that gender equality significantly decreased rates of women's homicide offending.[7] They defined gender equality through these indexes in legal, political, and economic terms. Best and Luckinbill (1990) found differences in the effect of gender equality when specific dimensions were observed. In their study, political and legal equality was more strongly associated with women's homicide offending rates than was economic or educational equality.

Best and Luckinbill (1990) also found gender equality more useful for explaining women's homicides that were nonfelony related. Given what we know about the context of women's homicide and the influence of gender equality in the domestic sphere, this finding makes sense. Felony-related homicide is characterized by a less domestic, more public interaction, which may be less affected by gender equality. Additionally, Browne and Williams (1989) found that the availability of resources for women, such as battered women's shelters, significantly decreased women's rates of homicide offending.

A compelling argument can be made that criminology must look closer at the effects of systematic gender equality and opportunity on women's homicide offending, incorporating both theoretical and empirical applications of gender equality to women who commit homicide. Despite public opinion and predictions by early gender and crime sociologists, equality and opportunity for women decrease rather than increase their rates of lethal violence.[8] In addition to the academic interest in gender equality and homicide, this kind of examination carries strong implications for policy and for ways society can begin to address women's homicide offending by improving women's lives.

Working from the basic concern for women's homicide and gender equality, the focus of this book is twofold: (1) to explore theoretically what it means to consider gender equality in explaining women's homicide offending and (2) to see empirically whether these gender-centered ideas help to explain the rates at which women kill, using the appropriate homicide data. This chapter has presented the case for studying women who commit homicide and why it is so important to include gender in such research. Chapter 2 considers the issue of gender and homicide theory, addressing first the application and shortcomings of traditional homicide theory with regard to women's homicide offending rates. The chapter then briefly examines theoretical perspectives on women and crime with regard to homicide and, finally, lays the framework for a gendered understanding of women's homicide rates overall and by type of victim. This creates a foundation for further discussion of gender structures and women who commit homicide.

Chapter 3 reports the results of macrolevel empirical analysis of women's homicide offending rates in cities. The data show that theoretical indicators derived from male experience and samples are unlikely to explain women's homicide as well as they explain men's.

Chapter 4 addresses the effects of low gender equality in intercity patterns of women's perpetration of homicide. Gender equality variables are first applied to women's homicide offending rates to examine what improvement gender inclusion makes in explaining why women commit homicide. Second, the best empirical models for women's homicide offending using both traditional and gender equality variables are derived and discussed.

Chapter 5 discusses how gender and gender equality concerns can extend beyond women's homicide offending. Application of gender equality to men's offending and, theoretically, to diverse groups further elucidates additional dimensions of the gender-homicide link.

Chapter 6 explores the implications and applications of the findings in this book concerning gender equality and women's homicide. This book is only a beginning for further work in conceptualizing and researching women's lethal violence, refining methodology, and considering policy and practical applications.

## Notes

1. Gender opportunities will be used as a synonym for gender equality. Gender system, macroanalytical gender relations, women's opportunities, gender stratification, and the like will be used to represent the relative state of women's disadvantage with regard to gender equality. Conceptually, a state of disadvantage for men would also be a state of low gender equality. At present, this could only apply to the social element of gender equality, and in this area both men and women are disadvantaged by the lack of freedom to pursue social roles and are subjected to differential normative expectations because of their gender. Given the position men hold in this society, however, even in this area men will wield more power than women. In all other ways, U.S. society has not reached an ideal of gender equality.

2. Some topics of gender studies writing have not been addressed here—including biological-reproductive inequality, spirituality, recreation, and the media—except insofar as they have overlapped economic, social, or political-legal equality. Considerations of biology and reproduction with respect to equality and homicide are beyond the reach of a social scientific study of women who commit homicide. Other cultural areas such as media, spirituality, recreation, and the like have a less direct impact on homicide

offending and in many cases have social or economic bases. Gender equality and its dimensions, as put forth here, should not be taken as a comment on or summary of the entire field of women's studies, gender studies, or feminism.

3. The term *fair* is used rather than *equality* because of some of the issues raised by MacKinnon (1987) with respect to the inherent inequality that can arise from so-called equal treatment under the law, which does not result in true equality. Instead, it results in a denial of protection and assistance for women on issues that incorporate key differences between men and women.

4. The connection between women's equality and homicide offending should not be overstated for women's homicides outside of the domestic sphere. As this analysis shows, acquaintance homicides do not decline significantly with relation to gender equality. The paucity of research on homicides committed by women against acquaintances and strangers and on felony-related homicides suggests we must exert caution in predicting that gender equality decreases all types of homicides despite the decline in overall women's homicide offending we have observed since around 1980.

5. The selection of large cities as the unit of analysis does not account for homicides in smaller cities and rural areas. Thus this discussion of gender and homicide reflects a focus on urban homicide. The applicability of theoretical conclusions from this book needs to be tested in different geographic locations to assess the large-scale generalizability of the gender-homicide connection.

6. Some caution should be exercised with such theorizing, as it is focused on victims presumed to be vulnerable to women's acts of violence. As the rate of family homicide considered in this analysis includes all family members, vulnerable and not, scenarios other than those involving children and elders do play out in women's homicide offending when it comes to family. Given that these groups constitute the vast majority of family homicide victims, however, the arguments here would apply theoretically to most homicide cases included in the data and considered theoretically.

7. The indexes used were previously established state-level measures. Best and Luckinbill (1990) used both David Sugarman and Murray Straus's Gender Equality Index and Kersti Yllo's Status of Women Index. Weisheit (1993) used only the Gender Equality Index. Further discussion of these indexes is given in Chapter 2, and a complete list of items is included in the notes to that chapter.

8. Equality for women has been met with the prediction that women will rise up, become more violent, and commit more crimes like men do. This belief is found not only in public opinion but in the writings of early scholars of women and crime such as Freda Adler (1975). We have not seen a rampant rise in women's violent crime since the beginning of the women's liberation movement. In fact, the rates of homicide committed by women remained stable during the 1970s and 1980s and began to drop from the late

1980s into the 1990s and up to the present (see, for example, Steffensmeier, 1993; Browne, Williams, and Dutton, 1999). The empirical observation that measures of gender equality are significantly and negatively associated with women who commit homicide would support the conclusion that actions to improve women's relative status would decrease women's homicide offending rates. Gender equality and opportunity may not have that effect with less serious forms of violence, and, as Rita Simon and Jean Landis (1991) and Steffensmeier (1993) have observed, rates of property crimes increased for women during this period. Exploring the connection between gender equality and opportunity for women and property crime is beyond the scope of this book.

# 2

## Approaches to Women's Homicide

Homicide theory has generally neglected issues of gender equality in women's homicide offending. When such theory has been applied, it has generally occurred in two distinct ways: (1) traditional theories have been applied to overall homicide rates and, by association, have been applied blindly to women, and (2) distinct theories of women's criminality have been extended to include women's homicide.[1] This chapter presents some primary concerns regarding theory, women's homicide, and gender. These concerns include the applicability of existing, traditional homicide theory for understanding women's homicide, the incorporation of homicide into general theories of women and crime, and the development of a gender equality–based understanding of women who kill.

### Gender Inclusivity and Generalizability: The Need to Examine Traditional Theory

Traditional homicide theory has developed without consideration of gender and has operated with an overall expectation that the same factors influence men's and women's homicide rates. The vast majority of homicide research has used traditionally derived predictors to explain overall homicide rates. As men's homicide offending is much more prevalent, analyses using total rates will more likely represent the factors affecting men's offending rather than women's. Although a few researchers (e.g., Steffensmeier and Haynie, 2000) have begun to examine gender-disaggregated homicide rates, the theoretical base on which macrolevel homicide study has been built has not been challenged. Thus the generalizability of the theory itself has not been fully assessed, and we cannot say how similar or dissimilar women's and men's homicide offending really is.[2] Darrell Steffensmeier and Dana Haynie (2000), in analysis of overall homicide rates for men and women, concluded that traditional variables are not as useful for understanding women who commit homicide as men who do so. They do not go very far, however, in revising existing theory to incorporate gender into the traditional explanations for homicide.

Additionally, subsuming gender within a total, aggregate rate allows us to see what homicide offending rates look like overall but not how well predictors explain women's homicide offending rates per se. As men commit homicide much more often, analyses using total rates more often represent the factors affecting men's offending. Thus it is unclear how similarly men's and women's homicide rates respond to those forces represented by homicide theory.

## A Feminist Critique of
## Traditional Homicide Theories and Women

Three major approaches have dominated homicide theorizing: inequality-deprivation, community disorganization, and cultural-subcultural explanations. As with other criminology theory, these explanations for homicide were developed without including women's perspectives and lives. These theories are discussed briefly to illustrate what insights may be left out when gender is not included.

### Deprivation Theory

Deprivation theory focuses on the effects of economic deprivation on communities. Research has demonstrated that areas characterized by high rates of poverty also have high rates of homicide (Messner and Rosenfeld, 1999; Williams, 1984; Williams and Flewelling, 1988; Parker, 1989; Land, McCall, and Cohen, 1990). The absolute deprivation argument maintains that the inability to provide for even the most basic needs produces stress and frustration that result in increased aggression and ultimately can lead to lethal violence. Absolute deprivation involves the most basic struggle for survival, which creates a demoralizing environment (Messner and Rosenfeld, 1999).

The economic deprivation perspective has not considered women's homicide offending or been examined for its ability to explain why women kill. Imbedded in this exclusion of women is the presumption that economic hardship is experienced for the same reasons and in the same ways by all persons, regardless of gender. This presumption ignores the potential impact of gender in two important ways: it fails to consider (1) access to economic resources and reasons for poverty and (2) the cultural meanings attached to those economic resources and poverty.

Feminist theorists have shown that, for example, men and women have very different positions relative to the capitalist economic structure. Men have been the primary participants in production and the marketplace, whereas women have tended to be the primary workers in the home—providing unpaid labor to support men and children (Abbott and Wallace, 1990; Fraad, Resnick, and Wolff, 1994; Williams, 1995). Thus men have generally been expected to provide the primary financial support for their families, whereas women's labor in the home has generally been unpaid and done for the benefit of the household. Women have traditionally provided emotional support in addition to household labor and have worked as auxiliary wage earners to make ends meet (Rubin, 1992, 1994; Abbott and Wallace, 1990; Messerschmidt, 1986).

Women's position in the capitalist economic structure is directly affected by discrimination, their devalued status as workers, and their lesser earning power than men (Rubin, 1992, 1994; Abbott and Wallace, 1990; Fraad, Resnick, and Wolff, 1994; Sidel, 1992; Ramazanoglu, 1989; Williams, 1995). Thus women are more likely than men to face economic deprivation through barriers to earning income outside the home. Further, public assistance inadequately compensates for women's disadvantage. Poor women have been supported more than men by public assistance, but such assistance is rarely sufficient to maintain even a minimal subsistence level. Additionally, stigmas from the degrading experience of working with public agencies and battling the public stereotypes of deviance in single-parent families often make public assistance a painful experience (Cook, 1987; Sidel, 1992, 1996).

The gender system provides structural barriers for women that make them more at risk for poverty. Additionally, the context in which women become poor differs from that for men. Men most often face poverty through unemployment, illness, or disability. Women most often become poor through the poverty of their male partners or through divorce, widowhood, or unmarried motherhood (Sidel, 1992; Rubin, 1992, 1994; Cook, 1987; Ramazanoglu, 1989; Chandler, 1991). Divorce hits women particularly hard. Lenore Weitzman (1985) found that particularly in no-fault divorces, equal splits of property seriously disadvantaged women who were often left with children and were forced out of the family home so it could be sold. The cost of raising children is rarely compensated by child support, which is often inadequate or goes unpaid (Weitzman, 1985; Sidel, 1992). The economic impact of poverty, then, can be very different for men and women (Steffensmeier and Haynie, 2000), which leads us to further question the exclusion of gender in many homicide studies.

The differential structural positions of men and women in the labor force are also associated with cultural meanings attached to earning money and financial status. Men's and women's respective relationships to production and income are highly associated with gender identity and related meanings. Simply put, earning money and acquiring material resources have different meanings for men and women. As primary providers, men have come to see the ability to earn money as an important part of being a man. Work is the core of self, and the ability to support one's family and have a profitable career are key parts of male identity (Rubin, 1994; Johnson, 1988; Abbott and Wallace, 1990; Messerschmidt, 1986, 1995; Taylor, 1991; Miller, 1985; Morgan, 1992).

The cultural importance attached to men's economic success has its roots in the family wage system, which decreased the need for women in the labor force by creating the male provider role (Messerschmidt, 1986). The significance of that provider role for men is felt when financial crisis occurs. Unemployment is seen as a threat to masculinity and results in shame and anxiety (Morgan, 1992; Levant and Kopecky, 1995). This impact can be intensified by the economic necessity of wives working for their families' survival rather than simply earning extra income (Rubin, 1994). Economic hard times, then, have the potential to cause frustration for men both in a practical sense and in a symbolic sense as a threat to identity and self-worth. Poverty thus has the potential to emasculate men and create environments in which masculinity must be demonstrated in other ways, including through violence and crime.

The cultural meaning women attach to work, economic resources, and poverty differs from that of men. Women respond to poverty more realistically than men (Pringle, 1995). Traditionally, for women identity has been more multifaceted, including many roles such as providing emotional and social well-being for the family in addition to managing the day-to-day economics of the home. Support of the family is primary for women, and emotional and social support is traditionally offered in exchange for economic support from the breadwinner (Mahoney, 1994; Rubin, 1992, 1994; Abbott and Wallace, 1990; Messerschmidt, 1986, 1995). Women's relationship to income and poverty is usually indirect, occurring through the spouse or partner who generally contributes the most money to the household and often maintains ultimate control of that money (Abbott and Wallace, 1990). For women, money traditionally represents the means to the end of providing support for the family, but it is not the core of most women's identities. Poverty, then, becomes less a threat to identity and more an obstacle to the ability to care for family needs (Pringle, 1995). Although women do receive satisfaction from working, employment serves the primary purpose of providing for the family. In short, economic hardship for women is more likely to result in other strategies for family survival and is less an identity threat than it is for men.

The absence of gender in economic deprivation perspectives on homicide leaves much ambiguity about exactly how poverty affects homicide and how gender can influence the poverty-homicide connection. The negative impact of poverty on men's lives and thus its effect on homicidal behavior is understandable, but we can question whether it would affect women's homicide rates the same way given the fundamental differences in men's and women's reactions to work and money. For women, poverty would be less likely to directly influence violence because it is less likely to invoke the need to demonstrate power and reinstate the value of self than is true for men. Any effects on women's homicide offending would likely be indirect, possibly through men's violence.

The fact that disproportionately high levels of women's poverty are not taken into account in traditional measurement provides a lack of empirical clarity as to how women's poverty influences the effects of economic hardship on homicide in general and on women's homicide in particular. The lack of empirical and theoretical considerations of gender makes economic deprivation perspectives unclear in their ability to explain women's homicide offending rates.

## Social Disorganization–Community Disruption

The social disorganization perspective is another theoretical approach to homicide that has not incorporated gender. This perspective, based on the neighborhood or community level, argues that particular ecological conditions in a community can result in higher rates of crime. Such conditions include high levels of population mobility, urban decay, poverty, decline in the strength of the family, and mixed racial-ethnic populations. These conditions lead to social disorganization, defined as a community's inability to articulate its values and recognize a common purpose. Social control fails, increasing the likelihood that residents will not behave in pro-community, law-abiding ways (Bursik, 1988; Kornhauser, 1978).

More recent work by Delbert Elliott and colleagues (1996) extends this perspective to demonstrate how a community's economic disadvantage combines with low levels of informal social control, low cohesion and consensus, lack of access to institutional resources, and illegitimate opportunity structures to make violence more likely. This work, though, does not incorporate gender any more than the original theory did.

Although the social disorganizational perspective originated to explain crime in general, homicide research has adopted some social disorganizational variables for study at the level of cities, states, and countries instead of neighborhoods. Social disorganization was theorized at the neighborhood level, so such use has provided some controversy (see Bursik, 1988). The percentage of the population who were black or African American has been used as a measure of heterogeneity.[3] Population density has been included as a measure of community economic deterioration (i.e., the impoverished are more likely to live in congested situations). The divorce rate has been used as a measure of family breakdown, and poverty has been included as a measure of community impoverishment. Of these indicators, the percentage of African Americans, the divorce rate, and poverty[4] have been the most consistent predictors of homicide as a whole.[5]

Social disorganization–community disruption arguments have

not included gender when explaining homicide. The empirical work of Ralph Weisheit (1993) found no significant correlation between a social disorganization index and women's homicide rates. In failing to incorporate gender, this perspective contains two assumptions: (1) men and women share the same communities that impact homicide, and (2) the features of community breakdown would operate similarly for men and women. These are questionable assumptions.

There is reason to question the concept of men's and women's shared community in a large sense. Women's networks tend to include intensive, kin-related, and children-related interactions. Men's networks, on the other hand, include interactions that are extensive, are based on jobs and careers, and are organized around information dissemination (Smith-Lovin and McPherson, 1993). The routine patterns of interaction and social influence for men and women would necessarily involve different levels and kinds of involvement in the community. Although the concept of community is critical in this perspective, the lack of attention to gender differences in community leaves the theory less able to explain women's versus men's homicide offending through those communities, which may be entirely different.

The nature and strength of women's communities deserve more discussion. The importance of family in these networks could have a strong impact on how community disorganization could affect women who commit homicide. Larger community forces such as poverty, heterogeneity, and population turnover could be mitigated by strong kinship support networks. Likewise, isolation from support networks can enhance women's distress and increase their likelihood to engage in lethal violence, a finding reported by both Jane Totman (1978) and Angela Browne (1987). At the same time, many women who are isolated and in the home do not have the benefit of those networks that provide independence and financial opportunity (Smith-Lovin and McPherson, 1993). If personal support networks, such as those provided by kin or fictive kin, are cut off, women are left in vulnerable positions with limited ways to cope and at greater risk of lethal violence. Social disorganization does not incorporate, and researchers have not directly examined, the nature of women's communities and their impact on women's homicide rates as a whole.

If a common community could be assumed, the lack of gender consideration in social disorganization theory carries the assumption that the breakdown of community affects men and women in similar ways. No empirical examination has been undertaken to see if this is the case, and no theoretical inclusion discusses gender in this context. Given the differential experiences and differential power and privilege of men and women, it is doubtful that the mechanism of social disorganization has the same impact for both genders.

The effect of divorce, as with all community disruption variables, has been assumed to be similar for men and women. Some studies, however, have found several differences between men's and women's responses to divorce. Men's health has been found to benefit from marriage (Miller, 1985; Fraad, Resnick, and Wolff, 1994). The emotional support and other care women often provide contribute much security and support to men. Some scholars have argued that in recent history women have become much more important to men emotionally than men have to women (Dennehy and Mortimer, 1993; Miller, 1985).

Research has consistently shown that divorce significantly increases overall homicide offending (e.g., Williams and Flewelling, 1988; Land, McCall, and Cohen, 1990). To make the argument that divorce has the same effect on men and women, however, one would need to presume that men and women respond similarly to divorce. This has not been the case. Men develop bonds with their spouses that serve as their primary emotional bonds and provide health benefits (Dennehy and Mortimer, 1993; Miller, 1985; Fraad, Resnick, and Wolff, 1994). Divorce provides a greater sense of long-term emotional loss for men, who are less likely to have intimate support networks (Albrecht, 1980). This loss can result in emotional instability, which can lead to violence. Women, on the other hand, suffer during the divorce but have more support from family and friends (Weitzman, 1985; Chandler, 1991; Smith-Lovin and McPherson, 1993). Thus divorce could more directly influence men's rates of homicide offending compared with women's.

Divorce, however, could also increase women's homicide offending rates, particularly those against intimate partners. The influence could be indirect through men's violence against women. Several researchers have found that men who kill current or former partners and spouses often do so when the woman actually leaves the relationship (Browne, Williams, and Dutton, 1999; Messner and Rosenfeld, 1999; Websdale, 1999; Browne, 1997; Browne and Williams, 1993). The majority of women's homicides are committed against intimate partners as a response to men's violence against them (Holmes and Holmes, 1994; Browne, 1987, 1997; Browne, Williams, and Dutton, 1999; Websdale, 1999). Thus divorce directly increases the risk of men's lethal violence, and it can also indirectly increase the risk of women's lethal violence through the response to that of men.

In general, the lack of gender consideration in social disorganizational perspectives on homicide makes the mechanisms through which disorganization affects homicide imprecise. These ecological-level variables could produce increases in both women's and men's homicide, but for different reasons. The connection between men's violence against women and women's self-defensive violence makes similar impacts unlikely. Social disorganization variables likely exert their influence on men directly and on women indirectly through their effects on men's violence against women. Social disorganization may be more useful for nondomestic homicide regardless of the gender of the offender. The dynamics of the intimate relationship and gender-based interaction within that relationship are also not addressed in this perspective. The community envisioned by social disorganization theorists was a more public arena in which intimate relationships would not be played out in general. In summary, the lack of gender and intimate context consideration results in a lack of clarity about whether and how social disorganization affects women homicide offenders.

## Cultural-Subcultural Perspectives

Cultural-subcultural explanations provide the third traditional perspective on homicide that has not incorporated gender. Cultural-subcultural arguments address the norms and values within particular communities associated with violence. This perspective covers two overlapping but somewhat different conceptualizations of subculture and culture. One, advocated by Marvin Wolfgang and Franco Ferracuti (1967), argues that subcultures exist in urban areas that are thought to accept and even promote the use of violence. The groups targeted in the literature as potentially violent subcultures have been African Americans and other minorities, the poor, and populations in the South because empirical correlations have been observed between areas with high numbers of these groups and higher levels of violence. The connection among minorities, the poor, and southerners in this perspective argues that they are particular groups characterized by an acceptance of violence, which is the link between them and violence.

In theorizing violence, the types of violence are unspecified. In research, the focus has been primarily on street violence and general homicide. Results from homicide analyses of the South have generally been mixed (Williams and Flewelling, 1988; Loftin and Hill, 1974; Messner, 1982; Corzine, Huff-Corzine, and Whitt, 1999), with fewer studies finding a relationship than not. Poverty has been more consistent (e.g., Williams, 1984). It is unclear whether poverty represents a subcultural orientation, a social disorganizational breakdown, or a structural inequality effect, as all three traditional perspectives argue the source of this relationship differently.

This first conceptualization of a violent subculture relies on a theorized connection between the numbers of persons in a particular social group and violent belief systems within that group. For example, a greater percentage of minorities in a geographic area was theorized to represent subcultural orientations supporting and encouraging violence among those minorities. Besides a lack of empirical support for the argument that such groups espouse more violent beliefs (see, e.g., Cao, Adams, and Jensen, 1997), this approach is generally weak and biased. In spite of that bias, the subculture of violence perspective has regularly included the South, minority populations, and poverty measures in homicide studies.

The second conceptualization of a subculture-culture of violence advocates a direct examination of belief systems and their connections to violence either at an individual level (e.g., Muehlenhard and Linton, 1987; Rapaport and Burkhart, 1984) or at the macrolevel (e.g., Williams and Flewelling, 1988). These conceptualizations have been more successful at connecting beliefs to violence and have been fairly successful in explaining homicide as a whole. Neither conceptualization of subcultures of violence, however, accounts for or examines gender. In fact, Wolfgang and Ferracuti (1967) distinctly stated that women are not violent and are not participants in violent subcultures. Their theory presumes that men are the only important participants in violent subcultures.

Few empirical studies have incorporated subculture of violence variables in their studies of women who commit homicide, and those that have (e.g., Weisheit, 1993; Mann, 1996) did not find support that the perspective applied to women's homicide. The exclusion of gender from the subculture of violence perspective makes two problematic assumptions: that (1) women accept violence as much as men do, and (2) women's violence would be as acceptable as men's within a violent subculture. These assumptions do not reflect what we know about men's and women's lives.

Regardless of subcultural membership, violent cultural orientation is relatively low for women, as evidenced, for example, in their low representation in homicide offending. Motherhood and the nurturing, caring behaviors that accompany being a mother are generally inconsistent with violent behavior. This identity and celebration of women as creators of life has been the center of women's participation in peace movements. Women's commitment to nonviolence in these movements has been active and vocal, and a connection between patriarchy and violence has been acknowledged (Ramazanoglu, 1989; Harris and King, 1989). Analysis of General Social Survey data by Liqun Cao and colleagues (1996) revealed that women were significantly less likely than men to accept violence in either self-defense or aggressive situations. Likewise, Sally Simpson (1991) reported that women were more likely than men to delegitimize violence, although that attitude may be more prevalent among white women than nonwhite women. Thus there is reason to question whether women are as likely as men to accept violence in general and particularly in the subcultures that have been theorized to be more violent.

In addition to the problem of assuming that women accept violence equally with men, the assumption that women's violence is equally acceptable to both genders is also questionable. A subculture that endorses violence may only accept men's violence. Controls and limitations on women's opportunities for illegal activities exist within deviant subcultures. Child rearing and household responsibilities keep many women homebound and out of high violence areas. These expectations, referred to by James Messerschmidt (1986, 1995) as emphasized femininity, place normative demands on women that emphasize nonviolence and nonaggressiveness. Illegitimate activities are often restricted by the subculture (Morris, 1987; Mann, 1984; Abbott and Wallace, 1990), and society stigmatizes deviant women who participate in violent, "nonfeminine" criminality with additional stigma and deviant labels. Even when women are allowed to participate in criminal subcultures, their roles are usually gender stereotyped. Male gangs, for example, usually place women in auxiliary roles, serving men's sexual and social needs and being the objects of, but not primary participants in, gang fights (Campbell, 1981; Jankowski, 1991). Thus the violence demonstrated by a subculture most likely reflects acceptability and demonstration of men's violence.

Clearly, gender has not been considered in the subculture of violence theory. This omission goes directly to the normative constraints and ideas that maintain the gender system.

## Women's Homicide Within Existing Feminist Approaches

The exclusion of gender in traditional approaches carries weaknesses in the ability to explain women who commit homicide. Theories that specifically address women's criminality have not offered thorough explanations of women's homicide offending. Many of these approaches confront issues of property crime and violence more generally, with much less attention given to women's homicide offending. These theories and their implications for women's homicide in particular will be discussed briefly.

### Liberation Hypothesis

One of the first theories about women's crime was advanced by Freda Adler (1975). In general, Adler reflected on a time of rapidly changing social norms for women and examined the effect of that change on women's criminality. Known generally as the liberations approach, the theory posited that women's crimes would increase as women were freed from traditional restraints and were allowed to take on more so-called masculine traits.

The basis for this theory was the observation that according to official arrest rates, women's crime rates were rapidly increasing. The increase was explained as resulting from the adoption of masculine behaviors by newly liberated women. Extended to homicide, the argument maintained that gender equality results in greater numbers of women committing homicide.

Despite gains in women's status in terms of employment, income, and legal and political representation, however, we have not seen the predicted increases in serious violent crime among women (Steffensmeier, 1993; Mann, 1984; Belknap, 1996; Abbott and

Wallace, 1990). For example, in an examination of women's homicide rates from 1960, 1975, and 1990, Steffensmeier (1993) found that those rates remained virtually the same over the time period (2 per 100,000 in 1960, 3 per 100,000 in 1975, and 2 per 100,000 in 1990). During that time, women's percentage of homicide arrests actually declined from 17 percent to 12 percent. Women's homicide has continued to decline, particularly intimate partner homicide offending (Browne, Williams, and Dutton, 1999). Additionally, little evidence suggests that women who commit crimes see the ideal woman as more masculine or are significantly more masculine themselves (Mann, 1984; Morris, 1987).

A possible reason serious violent offending has not increased is that gender equality, however defined, has not yet been achieved. For example, men and women are not yet paid equally for equal work, do not have equal access to power in the workforce and government, and are not equally free to fulfill social roles. Researchers have found little evidence that men and women have attained equality in power or resources (e.g., Williams, 1995; Wolf, 1999; England and Browne, 1992; Sugarman and Straus, 1988). The increases in serious violent offending predicted by liberations theory were predicated on such equality. Therefore, a true test of the predictions has not been possible, but all indications are that this theory will not hold, as women's offending has actually decreased as women have made gains in areas such as employment.

## Equal Opportunity Theory

Rita Simon (1975), although arguing that women's liberation would result in increased criminal involvement by women, did not argue that women's crime rates would increase across the board. As women gained greater access to the labor force and economic criminal activity, the theory argued, the rate of those crimes would increase. Women's participation in violent crimes, particularly homicide, was not expected to increase because new economic and social opportunities would decrease frustration and feelings of victimization and exploitation. Many homicides committed by women result from a move to eliminate the cause of dependence and subsequent frustration (i.e., men and children), so the elimination of subservient roles through women's liberation, it was believed, would remove the cause of most women's homicides. In later work, Simon (with Landis,

1991) stated that earlier observed trends in greater workforce participation and economic crimes continued, but violent crime did not.
The connection between gender equality, as social and economic
opportunity, and decreased women's homicide rates has been supported by later work examining women's homicide offending rates
(Weisheit, 1993; Best and Luckinbill, 1990). Simon's work lays the
preliminary groundwork for making sense of these findings.

### Frustration-Stress Arguments

Another theme in women's homicide offending is the frustration-
stress argument, which has also been embedded in other theories.
Simon (1975), although arguing that equal opportunities in the workplace were important in increases in higher-level economic crimes,
also argued that those same opportunities would decrease frustration
among women and, subsequently, violent crimes committed by them.
This attention to the role of frustration and social psychological
issues in understanding why women kill has led to other work. Anne
Campbell (1993) argued that women's aggression is primarily
expressive as a last resort to release built-up frustrations when efforts
to stifle them fail. Men, she argued, use instrumental aggression to
reassert control and achieve other goals.

A more recent theoretical argument, designed to explain
women's homicide per se, expanded on the social-psychological
foundations of frustration and stress. Robbin Ogle and colleagues
(1995) made the argument that the combination of baseline stress,
negative affect, blockage of coping mechanisms, and overstimulation
of situational stresses makes homicide more likely for a woman.
These forces are intensified by lower status. All women share baseline stresses from their structural, cultural, and social conditions in
society. This stress and devaluation are said to lead to low self-
esteem and negative affect. The authors argued that women share
blockages of coping mechanisms to alleviate stress and manage negative affect. Rather than deal directly with anger, women recast the
anger as guilt and turn their feelings inward. To cope, the authors
argued that women have developed overcontrolled personalities that
place powerful inhibitions on the expression of anger. Homicidal
women are said to suffer situational stresses that act as triggers.
Coping mechanisms break down, and as women do not learn the reg-

ulative rules of anger expression, anger gets out of control. Peaks of stress for women are more likely to result in an explosion, with episodes of extreme, uncontrolled violence aimed at those in the immediate environment—regardless of whether they are the actual source of the stress.

The theory advocated by Ogle and colleagues (1995) is a major step forward in theorizing women's homicide offending. Their focus at the level of the homicidal event provides several directions from which individual-level research can work. Although we know some of the situational correlates (e.g., abuse, threat, entrapment) of women who kill, we know much less about the process described in this theory.

Macroanalytical questions remain, however. First, gender equality is more of a backdrop to this theory than a variable in the analysis. Thus the impact of variation in gender equality and its association with women's homicide rates is not addressed and awaits further research. Additionally, the impact of structural factors is less defined, as their focus is more on individual women.

Existing theoretical approaches do not offer a complete treatment of women who commit homicide. Traditional perspectives ignore the influence of gender and thus may not explain women's homicide. Crime theories give some direction for understanding women's homicide offending but do not address gender equality in its full complexity. The first step to a fuller theoretical explanation of women who kill lies in gender equality. Its role in criminology will be discussed first as a foundation for its incorporation into a theoretical approach to women who commit homicide.

## Gender Equality in Criminology

Gender equality has been included in many criminology theories about women's offending, but it has been conceptualized in a wide variety of ways that have resulted in inconsistent definition and attention across these theoretical approaches. Additionally, the application of gender equality to homicide has not been clear in most theories.

The liberation theorists (e.g., Adler, 1975) directly consider one definition of gender equality, but they consider gender equality to be legal and economic equality defined as equal opportunity by law and increased women's labor force participation. Such gender equality, according to these theorists, would release women from gender role constraints so they could be more like men in their role playing. Equality was the achievement of liberation as a result of the women's movement. The lower the degree of gender equality, the more women are inhibited to commit violent crimes and engage in so-called masculine behaviors. The essence of this argument is one of control—that is, the root of crime and deviance is the lack of adequate social influences to draw women away from violent behaviors.

Opportunity theorists (e.g., Simon, 1975) make a similar control theory argument. If women had equal access with men to criminal subcultures and opportunities, they would be equally inclined to participate in violent and homicidal activity, they argue. Gender equality, then, is defined as equal access to criminal contexts. These two approaches have a narrow focus on what is viewed as gender equality.

Some researchers have conceived of a direct gender equality–homicide relationship in which some elements of gender equality are argued to lead to lower rates of women's homicide offending. Angela Browne and Kirk Williams (1989) argue that protective legislation and availability of shelters for battered women would lower women's homicide rates by allowing them to escape from abusive situations. These gender-based opportunities are operationalized as variables rather than static entities. Weisheit (1993) and Joel Best and David Luckinbill (1990), as we have seen, use measures that reflect an even broader conceptualization of gender equality that includes political, legal, educational, and economic dimensions. Their use of gender equality, however, is primarily empirical and is not expanded upon theoretically. Thus although they incorporate equality between men and women into their analyses, they do little to interpret their findings in the context of patriarchy. More general consideration of women's equality and the effects of opportunities is included in Ogle and colleagues' (1995) model.

The task for women's homicide theory development in this book is to conceptualize gender equality in comprehensive terms and to provide the basis for an operationalized measure that allows more direct observation of the relationship between the level of gender equality and women's homicide offending.

## Empirical Research Using Gender Equality

Translating gender equality into empirical criminological research has taken several forms. The first has been to view gender equality as a static state of affairs, something that "is," without operationalizing it. This is the form Ogle and colleagues (1995) and many feminist writers use. It is either "there" to be explored and detailed, or in the case of Ogle and colleagues' work, it is merely a backdrop to more individual-level processes. Unequal gender structures are used as background assumptions for individual-level theory. The portrayal of gender equality structures as a taken-for-granted assumption leaves us with several important questions, most important those that involve macrolevel empirical work where such representative concepts as women's labor force participation and percentage of single-parent households clearly vary by geographic location.

Empirical research has also used terms or indexes that try to capture levels of gender equality. As gender equality is a multifaceted and complex concept, any measure used to capture it must cover many areas. Some of the areas Dana Dunn and colleagues (1993) describe include access to valued resources and opportunities relative to men in all spheres of life, including material goods, services, education and training, decisionmaking, prestige, psychic enrichment and gratification, discretionary time, life-sustaining requisites, and freedom from physical coercion and behavioral restriction. Janet Chafetz (1991) also views gender equality as multifaceted and includes, additionally, food and medical care, prestige of roles, and power.

Feminists have built the framework of a gender equality system that encompasses virtually every aspect of humans' lives. Turning this highly complicated, multifaceted concept into a quantifiable, measurable construct is difficult. Each dimension of gender equality must have an operational definition based on data representing it that are available for analysis. Whereas economics, for example, may seem to be a fairly easy dimension given available census data, how does one measure social equality? When indicators are available, the weaknesses of secondary data inhibit the validity of these constructs. Many times in secondary data in particular, we are forced to use highly indirect measures that are open to differing interpretations. Additionally, one can only use what is available.

Two state-level indexes developed and applied to criminology meet many gender equality criteria: the Status of Women Index (Yllo, 1983) and the Gender Equality Index (Sugarman and Straus, 1988). Both indexes conceptualize women's equality in terms of gains made in economic, legal, and political spheres.[6] Kersti Yllo's index also includes an educational subscale.[7] These measures cannot incorporate all aspects of gender equality.

Social equality has not yet been operationalized in macrolevel analysis. Such indicators may be difficult to conceptualize, but measures of nontraditional living arrangements (unmarried households), women's divorce, and men's child rearing could shed valuable insight on the normative and value systems restricting or freeing women. Such variables would reflect the degree to which traditional values and norms of formal marriage and women's role as primary caregivers to children are emphasized. The more social freedom women have to live in nontraditional marital relationships, the less they will be restricted by expectations to be legally married and be subjected to the confining nature such relationships can have. If men and women share more of the child-rearing tasks, the demand that women do such work exclusively is reduced. As of yet, such social constructs have not been included in any macrolevel homicide research. Although state-level measures of gender equality have been developed in some of these areas, no measures currently capture this kind of gender structure at the city level.

Gender equality as a quantitative construct can vary. This means we can observe levels of achievement of a gender equality ideal that vary by geographic location. Sugarman and Straus (1988) found that states have a wide range of levels of gender equality, both overall and in terms of economic, legal, and political subindexes. States with higher degrees of gender equality were older, were more urban, had higher levels of socioeconomic status (SES), had more National Organization for Women members, and had less traditional attitudes toward sex roles. The finding that gender equality does in fact vary demonstrates the need to consider it as more than simply a constant. The point of such indexes is clear: gender equality is a viable construct in statistical analysis that requires consideration as a variable, not as static.

## How Low Gender Equality Affects Women's Lives

Living in a society with inequality of any sort is restrictive, frustrating, painful, and even potentially dangerous for those affected. This is the case with conditions of low gender equality, which is likely to restrict opportunities for social, economic, and political gains in devastating ways. When gender equality is high, women have more potential for freedom. The threat of women's equality *has* resulted in some backlash (e.g., Gartner, Baker, and Pampel, 1990, with regard to women's homicide victimization), but overall and in the long run high levels of gender equality will result in more freedoms for women.

### Effects of Low Economic Equality

Economic opportunities for women may be limited under conditions of low structural gender equality. With discrimination in the workforce and the lack of equity in pay, employment often fails to provide the same economic freedom it does for men. Women's work is often the lowest paid. Thus despite full participation in the labor force, many women must rely on the earnings of a man when the gender system is highly unequal. This problem has intensified with the deterioration of economic conditions for the working and middle classes since around 1970, which has eroded families' ability to live on one income.

The importance of women's need to rely on the earning power of men goes beyond the necessity of having adequate income for themselves and their families. As Clark Wolf (1999) and Philip Blumstein and Pepper Schwartz (1991) have found, dependence results from unequal pay and causes women to lack the power to make familial decisions. Low economic equality increases the likelihood of wage discrimination and sexism in the workplace and, when combined with the current economic status of the family, can result in significant disadvantage for women—particularly those who need to escape violence by intimates. The combination of a lack of power within the family and low wages tends to keep women in the home.

Thus the combination of wage discrimination, sexism in the workplace, and current economic conditions discourages women from remaining single or divorcing, even when they are married to someone who is abusive. The presence of children and the need to provide care for them intensifies economic dependence and other economic disadvantages. Therefore, in conditions of low economic equality, many women are trapped in less than ideal situations with little freedom to escape when necessary. The lower the degree of economic equality and opportunity for women, the more likely this is to be the case.

Single women with children are much more likely to be on public assistance than any other group. In general, the availability of public assistance is limited and declining (Sidel, 1996), and the amount given varies greatly. When women with children are offered Aid to Families with Dependent Children, food stamps, housing assistance, and the like, it carries a heavy price. The more low gender equality and stereotyping pervade a community, the greater the resistance to assisting women who "should" be married and relying on husbands to support their children (see also Chandler, 1991, for a discussion of the power of marriage ideology on women who are single). The stigma placed on women in these conditions is strong and increases as public opinion turns against those who are raising children in so-called unstable homes and are said to be creating new generations of juvenile delinquents (Sidel, 1996). Recent "welfare to work" initiatives have only intensified public scrutiny and criticism. These conditions undoubtedly increase the stress within these families. Thus from both a workforce and a public aid perspective, low gender equality can contribute to a serious lack of economic freedom for the majority of women, which can have serious and observable effects on the quality of women's lives.

### Effects of Low Social Equality

Low gender equality in social terms may also limit women's freedom and opportunities in ways less obvious but just as real. Social limitations include those core processes that define who we are and who we can be, what roles we play, and what behavior is appropriate. Gender polarities (as discussed previously and by such authors as Stoltenburg, 1999; Wolf, 1999; Chafetz, 1991, and others) result in strongly defined and enforced gender norms. Women who fail to adhere to submissive, passive behaviors are punished with stigma and other social sanctions (see Schur, 1984) and can even be penalized for such behavior in contacts with the police (see Visher, 1983).

Circumstances of low gender equality create conditions of general male privilege and power and can result in both the need for men to preserve their power position and the ability for them to do so. In fact, the need to achieve and maintain power is seen as a central and organizing principle in definitions and expectations of masculinity (Kimmel, 1996; Connell, 1995).

Social definitions of "maleness" and "femaleness" and "men" and "women" are the first and strongest protection of men's power under conditions of low gender equality. As discussed previously, many feminists have noted that women's status has revolved around their being thought of as "other" and "object," whereas men have been considered the subject and have been given primary importance (Klein, 1995; Coggeshall, 1991; Carlen and Worrall, 1987). This dichotomy creates a definition of status that is in binary opposition, in which everyone is required to fall into one of two categories with no recognition of behaviors or beings that fall in between. Being masculine requires rejecting anything defined as feminine (Messerschmidt, 1986; Connell, 1995). Defining men as not-women and women as not-men solidifies and reinforces patriarchal power, as by definition anyone not-men (including men who refuse to act like "men") is excluded from the privilege of being a man and from the legitimacy of men's power (Kimmel, 1996; Connell, 1995). The lower the degree of gender equality, the more likely this is to be the case.

The specific expectations that comprise being a man include adherence to hegemonic masculinity ideals—strength, ambition, aggressiveness, rationality, and lack of emotion—that are also valued traits in current society (Messerschmidt, 1986, 1993, 1995; Connell, 1995). Being a woman means being unlike men and being devalued and less respected than men. For example, John Coggeshall (1991) found that rape in men's prisons required that the victim—the dominated—be defined as a "woman." Masculinity as equated with dominance was thus supported and defined, and victimization through submission was defined as "feminine." Homosexual activity, normally taboo in the definition of masculinity, becomes accepted in prison when sexual aggression is redefined as "being a man" and the recipient of the aggression is transformed into a woman. The victim is thus no longer considered a man, and the act ceases to be homosexual. Instead, prison sex-rape is included in the expectations of men's behavior vis-à-vis women.

Although the previous example was a dramatic one taken from the prison environment, the cultural knowledge that supports this practice is much more broadly applied. For example, the use of names for women's genitalia (e.g., "pussy") or for women in general (e.g., "girl" or "sissy") constitutes a challenge to boys and men who do not conform to masculinity norms. Both Michael Kimmel (1996) and R. W. Connell (1995) discuss this verbal sanctioning as a means though which men are excluded from the power system for violating key masculine expectations. The greater the lack of equality between men and women, the more rigidly the social distinctions between "men" and "women" are made.

Gender roles and expectations follow close behind rigid definitions of men and women when gender equality is low. These rigid definitions restrict gender-typed behavior. As Edwin Schur (1984) described, gender norms are fiercely defended with the use of negative labeling, stigma, and other active controls. When gender equality is low, women are expected to be passive, to maintain traditional standards of appearance, and to welcome the opportunity to be a wife and mother. If they do not conform, they are labeled "butch," "ball buster," "lesbian," "spinster," and the like. Such labels and expectations limit the range of lifestyle choices and behaviors women can comfortably choose.

The formal criminal justice system can also become involved in strict definitions of womanhood. For example, Christy Visher (1983) found that traditional, passive behavior encouraged more lenient treatment by police, whereas aggressive and defiant behavior elicited harsher treatment. In general, scholars have found that women's aggression is more accepted when it is turned inward—as in alcohol abuse, drug abuse, suicide, and the like, which are more socially acceptable, passive forms of aggression for women. This direction is a direct result of gender expectations (see, e.g., Unnithan et al., 1994).

## Political-Legal Effects of Low Gender Equality

In political and legal terms, the lack of equality or fairness for women may result in major disadvantages in relation to law. Catharine MacKinnon (1987) has argued that the term *fairness* is more appropriate than *equality* because equal opportunity laws sometimes disadvantage women in arenas unique to them (e.g., maternity and childbirth). In an ideal legal system, men's differences would be considered equal to women's. MacKinnon believes women are disadvantaged by both a lack of equal protection laws in some places and equal protection laws that fail to consider some of women's specific needs. Without equal protection laws, women are targets of sexual discrimination and have no recourse to fight discrimination. When equal protection laws are in place, their enforcement is often literal, meaning men and women are treated—and expected to be—the same, even though women's reproductive and other domestic roles are not the same as men's.

When high levels of unfairness exist in the law, several effects follow. A lack of equal representation in legislative bodies means women's interests and protection are less likely to be at the forefront of lawmaking, whereas issues more often of direct concern to men get attention. As MacKinnon (1987) argues, though, representation itself does not automatically result in equal power. Without power, even large numbers of women representatives cannot get attention for women's issues. Even when men support women's issues, they cannot represent women's actual experiences. The lack of legal protection for women has serious consequences for women in unjust circumstances. For example, as a result of the reluctance to protect women legally from domestic violence, many women have been forced to endure serious abuse by partners without legal redress. When legal fairness and political equality are uneven with respect to creating law, women are less likely to receive assistance in such areas as abuse, child care, and the like. Conversely, where political and legal equality is higher, women are more likely to have equal political representation and power and legislation that protects and empowers them through equal opportunities and assistance to live the best lives possible.

An equal dimension of women's status in the political and legal system is the representation of women and women's issues among those who work in the criminal justice system. If the system has few female workers, women victims may not be able to turn to women for help and sensitivity.

Even if women are proportionally represented in the criminal justice system, as MacKinnon (1987) argued with respect to government, there is no guarantee that the system will be gender sensitive.

Even if women's protective legislation is in place and is enforced, a male-dominated criminal justice system can result in police officers' insensitivity and reluctance to enforce restraining orders and to arrest abusive men, for example. Mandatory arrest policies may be interpreted in ways least favorable to women. Even though mandatory arrest is based on the standard of "probable cause," some degree of officer discretion still exists. A gender-insensitive criminal justice system can also result in lower prosecution and conviction rates for perpetrators of domestic violence and lesser sentences for men who commit violence against women than for comparable nondomestic assault. A more gender-equal structure, on the other hand, will reflect equal legal protection and more equal treatment of all offenders and cases.

Low representation and influence of women can result in low government priority for institutions and programs devoted to women's assistance, such as battered women's shelters and publicly supported day care. Such assistance has not generally been a priority for male-dominated governments, where fewer persons can speak to women's experience and difficulties and address how such programs would be helpful. The class status of male legislators may insulate them from the day-to-day challenges faced by women because such men can often afford private day care and domestic assistance.

When women-centered programs are not a priority, as is characteristic in situations of low gender equality, the result can be a lack of support for women caring for dependents and a lack of ability for women to leave abusive situations. Shelters can provide safe havens for battered women and children to escape domestic violence. Public child care assistance can relieve some of the stress of child rearing and allow women more freedom to pursue outside lives and work that can provide a small degree of independence and self-improvement. A lack of support for these and other forms of assistance can reduce the opportunities and life chances for women outside the home.

Levels of gender equality have the potential to influence the lives of women in many ways. It is important to recognize that differences are also likely to exist in women's responses to gender equality. It stands to reason, then, that strong theoretical and empirical links will be found in the literature between the gender structures that influence women's lives and the type of lethal violence they commit.

## Gender Equality and Homicide

Low gender equality can have negative effects on women's lives in general. Many of the most extreme effects are manifested in the acts of women who kill. Several of the consistent and gendered themes in the empirical literature were presented in the introduction to this book. First, women are most likely to kill intimate partners, family members, and acquaintances. Second, a larger than average proportion of these homicides are victim precipitated (the victim provoked the attack), including by direct attack. Third, conflicts and quarrels are the most common motives for women's homicide. Most of these occurrences have been related to domestic situations typical of traditional women's lives.

A deeper theoretical case can be made for connecting gender equality and women's rates of lethal violence in direct and indirect ways. As we have seen, low gender equality can negatively impact women's freedom and opportunities, and these limitations can push women into situations in which lethal violence is seen as the only way out. Indirectly, a lack of equality for women combined with male dominance increases the legitimacy of men's violence against and coercion over women, as well as women's desire to please men—even those involved in criminal activity.

The preceding arguments for the link between gender equality and women's homicide offending apply in general to those homicides women are most likely to perpetrate. The importance of the victim-offender relationship, however, makes it necessary to discuss the precise theoretical connections between levels of gender equality and women's rates of homicide offending with regard to each type of victim-offender relationship. In the discussions that follow, that relationship is explored for women in general, but there may be differences among women in these categories—particularly in the dimensions of race-ethnicity, class, age, and other forms of diversity.

### Women's Domestic Homicide: Intimate Killing

Low levels of gender equality can be argued to have a direct bearing on women killing intimate partners. First, low levels of economic equality often limit opportunities for women to escape battering and other abusive situations. Lack of employment means abused women are less likely to be able to separate from or divorce their spouses and thus escape the likelihood that the violence will escalate into a lethal situation. Many women stay in such situations only because they are unable to make enough money to support themselves and, often, their children. Additionally, the economic and decisionmaking power in families is more unequal when only one person (usually the man) works. The lower the income of women relative to men, the less likely it is that women's paid labor outside the household will be seen as desirable and the more likely it is that women will remain in the household without the power independent income brings. Several scholars have identified a lack of economic resources as a key factor in keeping women in abusive situations (Yllo, 1993; Belknap, 1996; Abbott and Wallace, 1990).

Lack of social equality increases the likelihood that women will remain in abusive relationships because traditional gender norms dictate that legal marriage is the only appropriate long-term romantic relationship (see Chandler, 1991). Also, traditional norms generally place responsibility on women to please men and require that women be submissive, docile, and accepting of whatever their husbands do because they are the dominant partner (Hampton and Coner-Edwards, 1993; Carlson, 1987; Abbott and Wallace, 1990). These beliefs, held by both men and women, stigmatize women's separation and divorce and deny legitimacy to nonmarital, cohabiting relationships. In low gender equality, marriages are more likely to be considered to be the responsibility of women. In a traditional gender system women may see the breakup of a marriage as shameful, stigmatizing, and a personal failure (Carlson, 1987; Bowker, 1993). Acceptance of women's divorce or separation and cohabitation provides more power for women who can then leave marriages and be in relationships without legal constraints should the situation become abusive. Lack of acceptance, on the other hand, emphasizes being and staying legally married despite what men may do in such relationships.

Research presented thus far indicates that low gender equality may decrease or eliminate women's economic and social opportunities to escape abusive situations. Additionally and equally important, a lack of gender equality may encourage the abusive situation in the first place. Patriarchy provides ideological support and legitimation to men's dominance in families and to the violent means used to maintain that dominance (Hampton and Coner-Edwards, 1993; Gondolf, 1993; Yllo, 1993; Ferraro, 1988; Abbott and Wallace, 1990;

Ramazanoglu, 1989, Pagelow, 1981a, 1981b; Kurz, 1989; Greenblat, 1983; Bograd, 1988; Browne, 1997).

Historically, men have been held legally accountable for the actions of their family members (Taylor, 1991; Carlson, 1987). Traditionally, domestic disputes have not been considered a police matter. Prosecutorial action and sentencing in domestic cases have been less severe than those for similar charges for victims outside the family (Holmes and Holmes, 1994). Physical punishment and control over women and children have often been considered part of the privilege of being the man of the family. The concepts of wife battering and marital rape did not gain public or legal recognition until well after feminists in the 1970s increased awareness and campaigned aggressively for change. Even with recent changes in legislation (such as the federal Violence Against Women's Act of 1994), change has been slow to come and has varied across jurisdictions.

Evidence indicates that acceptance of the macrosystem of patriarchy and male privilege, indicative of low levels of gender equality, is a key background factor in individual accounts of battering. Messerschmidt (1986, 1993, 1995) has argued that violence is an accepted, often expected way to enact masculinity and establish dominance over women (see also Viano, 1992). High adherence to and acceptance of traditional gender roles have been found in batterers (Browne, 1997; Saunders, 1992; Gondolf, 1993; Ferraro, 1988; Pagelow, 1981a, 1981b; Dutton and Golant, 1995; Smith, 1990). As the arguments made by criminologists such as Messerschmidt (1993) indicate, violence as a way of enacting masculinity becomes most likely when dominance is threatened. One such threat arises when women have higher social or economic status than men (Smith, 1990; Rubin, 1994; Carlson, 1987). Kathleen Ferraro (1988), Angela Browne (1987, 1997), Martha Mahoney (1994), and others describe violence by male partners as more likely when a strong symbolic threat exists to his sense of self and dominance. One crucial threat to men's dominance is separation or the threat of separation. This event has been described as a primary instigator of domestic violence, often more severe than women had experienced prior to the threat of separation (Bowker, 1993; Browne, 1987, 1997; Dutton and Golant, 1995).

Low levels of gender equality can increase the emphasis on traditional gender norms and thus increase the threat to masculinity, in particular when dealing with the challenge posed by a woman in an intimate relationship. We can then postulate that low levels of gender equality can also be a factor in creating abusive situations that may result in women's use of violence as a self-defensive action. This context hinges on the patriarchal expectations and ideologically supported actions of men who are seeking to preserve their power in relationships.

The question remains, when does homicide become the preferred action? We know that the vast majority of women who kill intimate partners do so in response to abusive situations, often in imminent self-defense or when other strategies have failed (Ferraro, 1997; Belknap, 1996; Saunders, 1986; Gillespie, 1989; Stout, 1991; Kelly, 1996; Chimbos, 1978; Totman, 1978; Walker, 1989; Browne, 1987, 1997). Women engage in suicidal behaviors more often than in homicidal behaviors (Unnithan et al., 1994), showing that their aggressive feelings and negative emotions are generally more likely to be turned inward.

Ogle and colleagues (1995) argued that a period of increasing stress occurs prior to killing and that management of negative affect breaks down. With respect to intimate partner abuse, a cycle of violence has been described that includes escalating severity and increasing frequency of violence that could definitely produce such stress (Walker, 1989; Dutton and Golant, 1995). Some researchers who have studied women who kill abusive partners have found that this period of increasing stress exists before the homicidal incident. Threats to kill by the abusive husband are frequently made in the period before the homicide. As women perceive their own or their children's well-being to be in jeopardy, they are more likely to act defensively against the partner. Women who have killed their partners have described a strong sense of "it's him or me" and "this is the one," meaning they knew that the particular incident would result in their death if they did not act (Browne, 1987; Walker, 1989). Steven Messner and Richard Rosenfeld (1999) called this threat of women's homicide victimization the most extreme form of men's domination and attempts to control women.

As such violence continues and intensifies, women begin to realize that they will die if no action is taken. Because of an inability to act during the most acute phase of the beating, some women wait until their partners are incapacitated by sleep or the use of intoxicants or have their backs turned before they act. Additionally, many equalize the strength differential by using guns (Gillespie, 1989).

In summary, intimate partner homicide is directly influenced by low levels of gender equality. This occurs through limited economic opportunities, which prevent women from leaving abusive relationships, and failure of human service institutions to provide options for women to escape from domestic violence situations. Gender equality, on the other hand, can decrease both the legitimacy given to men's violence against women and the number of situations in which women will need to use self-defensive action by providing support and opportunities to leave abusive relationships.

## Domestic Homicide:
## Children and Other Family Members

The other primary group of women's victims includes children and other family members. These homicides can be seen as largely a function of low gender equality and its effects on women's lives.

Lack of social gender equality may play heavily in the dynamics of child killing. The lack of such equality and the presence of male dominance are likely to result in traditional expectations regarding women's role in the home and the structure of the family in general. These expectations and structures are likely to be characterized by low levels of power for women vis-à-vis men, which will probably result in a restrictive domestic situation. Traditionally, working- and middle-class women have been responsible for child rearing and been left at home alone to raise children. Greer Fox and Jan Allen (1987) have argued that traditionally, childbearing justifies a woman's place in family and society and is both highly normative of and demanded by that society. Children are often expected to be the center of a mother's life, whereas men's parenting is often considered secondary to wage-earning roles. Child rearing has been just one of the many household duties of traditional housewives, none of which is usually financially compensated or externally rewarded. Thus raising children is unpaid labor from which the men and the children generally benefit most. Child rearing in itself is not oppressive or restrictive, but the patriarchal demand that women do this work and do it without assistance raises the likelihood of associated stress.

In addition to the demand that women should be the primary caregivers of children, they are often expected to do so alone. The woman in a highly patriarchal society is expected to manage the competing demands she faces from her family quietly and without complaint (Fox and Allen, 1987). She often does so in isolation and without support (Klein, 1995). The use of child care in such societies is viewed as deviant, harmful, and threatening to the sanctity of the family (Fox and Allen, 1987).

The more traditional the view, the more negative the perception of child care and other assistance. Women are stigmatized for leaving children in the custody of others, as a "good" mother would stay home with her children. Stigma can also come from within if women feel guilty for leaving their children so they can work and engage in other activities. This is also a result of the traditional belief that good mothering should not be compromised by wage earning (Fox and Allen, 1987). Thus opportunities to deal with the stresses and problems of child rearing are limited by the expectation that "good" mothers will stay home with their children. This inflexibility in gender roles has been identified by Leslie Margolin (1992) as one factor that encourages women's child abuse.

A single parent is likely to feel this stress even more intensely. Without a partner to help at home, the single parent often feels more burdened, with a lack of personal time. Additionally, the presence of children can decrease a woman's chance of remarriage and negatively impact career mobility, as her free time and loyalty are devoted to her children rather than to dating or extracurricular, career-oriented activities. If a woman does spend time on such things, she may be labeled a poor mother and her custody may be challenged.

Traditional normative demands also include the expectation that women will have children within the institution of marriage. Infanticide has been found to be strongly associated with illegitimacy and the stigma of having children out of wedlock (Weisheit, 1986; Silverman and Kennedy, 1988). Robert Silverman and Leslie Kennedy summarize: "They probably see no options except to kill a child—to avoid discovery, to avoid shame and stigma for themselves and their family" (1988: 125). The expectation that women have children within marriage is clearly derived from the traditional normative gender structure that supports patriarchy and its low level of gender equality. A society characterized by low gender equality is less likely to accept single motherhood, a strong factor that may increase the chance that a woman will kill her offspring.

Economic gender equality also has a role in understanding why women kill family members. A lack of economic equality can negatively impact women with children. Messner and Rosenfeld (1999) found direct evidence that economic stress was linked to infant homicide victimization and that increased social spending decreased child homicide. Neil Websdale (1999) also described child homicide as highly associated with poverty, inequality, and economic marginalization. Given that women are most vulnerable to economic stress when high gender inequality exists, these findings indicate that conditions of low economic equality will increase women's likelihood to live in poverty without assistance and thus increase the risk that they will kill their children.

Further support for the connection between economic stress and violence is found in the area of child abuse. Research has shown that a lack of economic resources increases the chances of child abuse occurring (National Research Council, 1993; Milner and Crouch, 1993; Gelles, 1993). In fact, the National Research Council (1993) stated that "mothers living below the poverty line have the greatest risk of behaving violently toward children" (9). Having economic resources has been found to mitigate against the negative impact of familial stress (National Research Council, 1993; Milner and Crouch, 1993).

Women who kill children are often seen as acting out an extension of child abuse, and thus it is not surprising that economic deprivation, financial strain, or other economic loss are often present for those women (Totman, 1978; Ogle, Maier-Katkin, and Bernard, 1995; Holmes and Holmes, 1994; Weisheit, 1986; Mann, 1993). Women are more likely to be in these economic situations when gender equality is low because of the greater likelihood of their being in devalued and underpaid positions in the labor force and of being single parents with custody.

Low social and economic gender equality and traditional notions of family can affect caring for other family members. Traditionalism, characteristic of low social gender equality, carries very strong prescriptions concerning the sanctity of family and the loyalty one should have for family members. Historically, families have rarely used facilities and home nursing to care for aging relatives. The onus of responsibility for their care has generally rested on younger members of the family, specifically the younger female members (Steinmetz, 1993). In fact, more than 80 percent of elder care is estimated to be provided by women. The necessity of placing aging or disabled family members in a nursing home or other such facility can carry guilt and conflict that can divide families and cause great stress. Refusal to provide care often receives little support, and further, the provision of care is taken for granted and assumed to be easy (Hooyman and Ryan, 1987). Many women still care for elderly family members because of feelings of loyalty and the high costs associated with such care.

Caring for disabled or aging relatives can actually be very stressful. Medicines, treatments, trips to physicians, and basic needs must constantly be monitored. Men as a rule do not perform these functions but are involved indirectly by providing finances and home maintenance; they provide hands-on care for the elderly only when a woman is unavailable (Hooyman and Ryan, 1987). Time to oneself is a luxury available only when someone else takes over the caregiving tasks and many women caring for relatives do not have such assistance. As a result, women who provide such care cannot release stress effectively.

The economics of elder care can be problematic for women as primary caregivers. Increasingly, families are expected to provide the cost of care for older relatives without compensation for their services. For women providing care, employment outside the home is usually not possible. Many women caregivers are so economically deprived that Nancy Hooyman and Rosemary Ryan (1987) state, "Yet even those who give first priority to caregiving tasks are frequently punished by poverty and powerlessness" (144). Caregivers are often faced with low earning power in the workplace, and many choose to leave work to give full-time care because of gender-based inequities in pay for the work they are able to do (Hooyman and Ryan, 1987).

Elder abuse is found to be associated with the stresses of caring for elders. These include psychological exhaustion, subsuming individual needs to the needs of the elderly family member, devaluing the caregiving, and financial strains involved in caregiving (Boudreau, 1993; Steinmetz, 1993; Finkelhor and Pillemer, 1988). The less others are available to assist, the greater the dependency of the elder on a single caregiver, and the greater the degree of dependence, the more likely it is that abuse will take place (Steinmetz, 1993). Elder homicide, as an extension of abuse, is likely affected by these elements.

Women's relationships with children and elders share several important factors. The first is the social demand, in more traditional social systems, for women to care exclusively for both the very young and the elderly. The second common element is the frequent deviantizing of women caregivers seeking outside help such as child care or nursing home care. The third common factor is the economic strain such caregiving often causes and the negative impact of women's disadvantage in the workforce on the economic costs of caring for elders or children.

From these common background dynamics, we can develop theory about the homicidal situation. Although research provides less information about the killing of nonintimate family members than it does about intimates, some cues from the triggers of intimate homicide and the dynamics of child and elder abuse can create a theoretical picture of what happens.

Emotional stress has been identified as a major trigger in child abuse (Milner and Crouch, 1993; Gelles, 1993), elder abuse (Boudreau, 1993; Hooyman and Ryan, 1987; Finkelhor and Pillemer, 1988), and the killing of children (Holmes and Holmes, 1994; Totman, 1978; Weisheit, 1986; Silverman and Kennedy, 1988). It is unlikely, however, that stress alone causes a homicidal event. Stress, when combined with a lack of social and economic support and extreme isolation, can lead to a state in which options are seen as limited. Totman (1978) described child murder offenders as feeling confined and having little meaningful interaction outside the home. Social isolation and feelings of entrapment were also reported in child abusers (Milner and Crouch, 1993) and elder abusers (Steinmetz, 1993; Hooyman and Ryan, 1987). These problems are compounded by the dependency of the child and the elder on the caregiver.

The effects of isolation and limitations of social options can be intensified by a lack of economic resources to obtain necessary assistance. In both child abuse studies (Milner and Crouch, 1993; Gelles, 1993) and elder abuse studies (Boudreau, 1993; Gelles, 1993; Hooyman and Ryan, 1987), limited economic resources interacted with subjective experiences of stress to make abuse more likely. If these familial homicides are viewed as a lethal extension of abuse, a picture emerges of women as more likely to kill when they are expected to be the sole caregivers and to sacrifice their own needs, when they are experiencing stress from caregiving demands, when they are isolated, and when they receive little financial assistance. Low levels of gender equality increase the likelihood that women will experience these conditions.

The homicidal event will likely be a final effort to escape from a seemingly inescapable situation. Like her intimate partner homicide counterpart, the female familial homicide offender will kill the perceived object of her oppression. As N. Prabha Unnithan and colleagues (1994) discuss, in lethal violence the choice of homicide occurs when the source of one's stress and anger becomes externalized and located outside the self. At this point aggression will be turned toward that perceived source. It is at this point that the killing of children and family members is most likely to happen, particularly if no other alternatives are seen for alleviating the stress. Totman (1978) reports that children who were killed were viewed by their mothers as irritants and as symbols of frustration, boredom, confinement, and failure. There is also a sense that abuse (and, by extension, killing) of the powerless is fed by a woman's own powerlessness and represents a desperate attempt to gain power for herself. The roots of this powerlessness can be seen as stemming in part from a society that does not offer women equality with men.

The general features of gender equality may operate in these specific types of family killing. Other forms, such as homicide by siblings, are not addressed here. The potential effect of gender equality is unknown for these rarer types of women's family homicide.

### Acquaintance and Stranger Homicide

Stranger homicide is very rare, and the majority of women's homicides are the result of conflict and not of felonies or seeking economic gain (see Chapter 1). Because so little is known about acquaintance and stranger homicides committed by women, they are difficult to explain. There are two possibilities. First, a degree of gender equality is probably a factor in these types of homicides. As low levels of gender equality promote traditional gender roles and the subordination of women, we can reason that women accomplices become involved in homicidal activity because of the needs, desires, or demands of the men with whom they are involved. This is indeed a theme among women involved in crime in general. As one researcher's ethnographic contact with homicidal women in prison revealed, to preserve a relationship and take care of her man, a woman may take the blame for him, be coerced or encouraged to help him do a heist, or otherwise become involved in his criminal activities (Jensen, 1990). Also, because of inequities of power in the relationship—a feature of low gender equality—a woman is also at risk of emotional and physical coercion to help him.

In addition to possible pressure to assist in male-directed activity, defense of family can also be an outgrowth of traditional gender values associated with inequality. The same researcher's ethnographic contacts with women in prison revealed that a woman had sometimes killed a stranger or an acquaintance because she believed her children were in danger or felt the need to execute vengeance for some wrong done to her family (Jensen, 1990). Such protection by a mother and defense of family is consistent with traditional gender expectations that a woman should place family members first, even before her own safety.

A second consideration in theorizing the macrolevel picture of women who kill acquaintances and strangers is the equally likely possibility that men's and women's homicides may appear more similar than different. The context surrounding the killing of acquaintances and strangers involves a more public sphere than that of domestic homicides. The former are more likely to take place in public establishments (such as bars), on the street, and in the workplace. These situations may be more removed from the effects of low gender equality than is true in the home. Women are much less likely to commit homicides in this public sphere, and once this separation has been removed, women are more likely to be influenced by criminal subcultures and other features of public life. The structural features of the public environments in which acquaintances and strangers are killed may affect men and women similarly once women are exposed to these public worlds. Thus women who kill outside the home may be more similar to their male counterparts than they are to their female domestic homicide counterparts. These dynamics have not yet been addressed in research and theory development, and women's acquaintance and stranger homicide requires further study.

## Gender Equality Research Hypotheses

From the theoretical discussion presented here, we can extract several key hypotheses:

*Comparing Men's and Women's Homicide Offending/Testing Generalizability*

1. Traditional theories of homicide will explain women's homicide offending rates less successfully than men's rates.
2. Individually, traditional predictors will be more successful in explaining men's homicide offending than women's. Significant differences will be found that show that the predictors are stronger for explaining men's homicide offending.

*Gender Equality*

1. Social and economic equality will greatly enhance our ability to explain women's homicide offending using traditional homicide models, especially those homicides that reflect women's traditional positions: intimate partner and family.
2. Social and economic equality will decrease women's homicide offending; this will be seen in intimate partner, family, and overall rates (because of the inclusion of domestic homicides). Equality will have little effect on acquaintance homicides because of the low likelihood that these homicides occur as a result of stress induced by low gender equality.

## Notes

1. Ogle and colleagues (1995) do present a specific theory of women's homicide. The primary focus of their theory, however, is on psychological and social psychological influences on individual women, and it does not directly address social structures, particularly those that relate to gender inequality.

2. Kathleen Daly and Meda Chesney-Lind (1988) were the first to identify the "generalizability problem" in the field of criminology. According to these authors, most criminological theories have been derived from young male samples and have never been tested for their usefulness in explaining female criminality. Whereas this has been the case in general, it particularly applies to macrolevel criminological analysis. It should be noted that some research using self-reported data on delinquency has claimed to be more gender inclusive, as the empirical research has included gender as a variable in analyses considering bonding, parental controls, and other individual-level factors in delinquency. See, for example, Elliott, Huizinga, and Menard (1989); Gold and Reimer (1975); Gold (1970); Elliott, Huizinga,

and Ageton (1985); Elliott and Huizinga (1983); Thornberry et al. (1994); Smith and Thornberry (1995); Krohn et al. (1992).

3. The use of this percentage of African Americans as a measure of heterogeneity has problems. Heterogeneity as a concept has its highest values at the middle of a curve when the mix is around 50 percent. The use of this measure as a linear function may represent not the mix presumed in heterogeneity arguments but some other feature of the nonwhite group used in the equation.

4. The interpretation of poverty in the social disorganizational framework differs from that of the deprivation framework. Whereas deprivation argues that the central problem is a stress individuals in poverty feel, social disorganizational theory argues that poverty has an effect on the community or neighborhood that decreases the desirability of the area through disorder and dilapidation, which discourages residents from forming ties within that community. Delbert Elliott and colleagues (1996) also point to the lack of resources for that community and the rise of illegitimate opportunity structures, such as prostitution and drug dealing.

5. Direct measures of community breakdown at the city or state level have not been developed. Studies have been unable to address directly the community and social control that underlies this theory. There is really no such measurement, particularly not one we could apply to cities or other levels of aggregation. The predictors discussed here reflect features of a neighborhood that may affect this breakdown but do not directly measure it. Instead, these proxy measures are more reflective of symptoms of the problem. The use of these indicators does, however, extend throughout the homicide literature.

6. This is a complete list of Gender Equality Index items (Sugarman and Straus, 1988).

*Legal Equality Subscale Items:*
State passage of fair employment practices act
Allowing women to file lawsuits personally under fair employment practices act
State passage of equal pay laws
Allowing women to file lawsuits personally under equal pay laws
State passage of laws preventing discrimination in public accommodations, housing, financing, education
Statutes that require civil injunctions providing relief for victim abuse
Physical abuse of family or household member considered criminal offense
State permits warrantless arrest based on probable cause in domestic violence cases
State requires data collection and reporting of family violence by agencies that serve those families

State provides funds for family violence shelters or establishes standards of shelter operation

*Economic Equality Subscale Items:*
Percentage of women participating in civilian labor force relative to men
Percentage of women who were managers and administrators relative to men
Percentage of women employed relative to men
Median income of women relative to men
Percentage of Small Business Administration loans given to women compared with men
Percentage of Small Business Administration money loaned to women relative to men
Percentage of female-headed households above poverty level relative to male-headed households

*Political Equality Subscale Items:*
Percentage of state senate members that were women
Percentage of state house members that were women
Percentage of mayors that were women
Percentage of governing boards that were women

7. This is a complete list of Status of Women Index items (Yllo, 1983: 282–283).

*Legal Subscale Items:*
No occupations barred to women
Equal pay laws
Fair employment practices act
No maximum hours restrictions for women
Proof of resistance not required for rape convictions
Corroborating testimony not required for rape convictions
Husband and wife jointly responsible for household
Husband and wife have an equal right to sue for personal injury
Husband and wife have an equal right to sue for loss of consortium
Wife's property rights unrestricted
Wife's right to use maiden name unrestricted
Wife's right to maintain a separate domicile unrestricted
State ratified federal Equal Rights Amendment
State passed state Equal Rights Amendment

*Economic Subscale Items:*
Percentage of women in labor force
Percentage of women in professional and technical professions
Percentage of women in managerial and administrative occupations
Men's unemployment rate as percentage of women's rate

Women's median income as percentage of men's for full-time workers

*Political Subscale Items:*
Percentage of U.S. Congress members that are women
Percentage of state senators that are women
Percentage of state house members that are women
Percentage of major appellate and trial court judges that are women

*Educational Subscale Items:*
High school education—women's rate as a percentage of men's rate
Percentage of postsecondary enrollment of women
Percentage of women participating in high school interscholastic athletics
Percentage of women in high school administration

# 3

# Gender and Homicide: Comparing Men and Women

Chapter 2 theoretically explored the importance of gender and gender equality in explaining women's homicide offending. The empirical portion of this book addresses two major questions about women who commit homicide. First, how does women's homicide offending differ from that of men? This question is addressed in two ways. First, this chapter looks at the distribution of homicides by gender overall and by victim-offender relationships, and second, it examines some of the traditional homicide predictors applied to women's and men's homicide offending rates separated. The second question, addressed in Chapter 4, considers the value of adding gender equality variables to explain women's homicide offending rates. Given that women and men differ in their patterns of homicide and given women's disadvantages in a patriarchal system, gender equality provides the most promise for a more complete explanation of rates of women's killing.

Examination of the homicide data, except for descriptive statistics, will focus on overall homicide rates and for victimization of intimate partners, family members, and acquaintances—broken down for both men's and women's homicide offending rates. There are two primary reasons for the focus on these victim-offender contexts. First, the choice of contexts is limited to those categories that have sufficient homicide incidents for rate construction. As women rarely kill strangers, it was not possible to examine women's stranger homicide rates; thus men's rates of killing strangers could not be included in the comparative analysis.

A second reason for looking at these particular victim-offender relationships is to examine homicide patterns that can differ greatly because of different levels of intimacy. In particular, it is important to examine differences in relationships because theorizing about gender equality and women's homicide offending highlights the important effects of gender in women's lives, especially in the context of intimate relationships.

## Data and Methodology

The analyses of homicide offending rates for women and men are drawn from the FBI's 1990 Supplementary Homicide Reports (SHR). The SHR is part of the FBI's annual Uniform Crime Reports (UCR) program and gives information on homicides known to the police regardless of whether an arrest has been made. Homicides are defined as murder and nonnegligent manslaughter offending, as included in the SHR for the 200 cities and census-designated places that had census-listed populations of 100,000 or more. After the exclusion of cities not reporting homicide to SHR in 1990, 179 cities remained in the sample.[1]

Large cities were used for two reasons. First, it is necessary to select a unit of analysis that reflects the level of the theory from which variables are derived. Social disorganization and deprivation theory in particular addresses community-level dynamics. Therefore cities reflect the most appropriate unit of analysis for this kind of study.[2]

Second, the selection of large cities as the unit of analysis represents the greatest variability possible with a level of analysis large enough to support the creation of homicide rates, calculated as the number of homicides committed per 100,000 men or women, depending on which homicide rate was being calculated. Potential intercity variation is greater than interstate variation, which gives us a greater ability to test theory and take into account important differences between cities within states—particularly large states like Texas, New York, and California.

The analysis was organized around two primary research questions: Do traditional explanations of homicide explain men's and women's homicide equally well, and how much do measures of gender equality improve upon these traditional predictions to explain women's rates of homicide offending?

## Measuring Traditional Variables

The traditional measures used for the comparative analysis were derived from social disorganization and deprivation and subculture of violence theories. The measures used were also those frequently used by others in conducting homicide research. The percentage of African Americans was incorporated to represent heterogeneity, mainly in keeping with other research that has used the measure. This measure is incomplete because it does not incorporate other kinds of diversity. Other community disorganizational and deprivation variables included the percentage of families in poverty, the percentage of population change between 1980 and 1990, and population density, measured as the number of people per square mile. These are not perfect indicators of theory but have been standard in many other studies of homicide and, as a point of comparison, are included here as well. Overall family instability was measured using the number of divorced and separated persons as the basis for calculating the percentage of those divorced or separated. The South was used as a dichotomous, dummy variable with a score of 1 given to cities that were in Confederate states. This indicator is used as a proxy for a southern subculture of violence, but there are no real measures of an actual subcultural belief system. All traditional predictors, except the South, were taken from the 1990 U.S. Census.

## Measuring Gender Equality

Creating measures for gender equality was a challenge. As with all secondary data, researchers are limited to what has already been gathered. To a large extent, the census provides data on cities. It was impossible to develop indexes like those created by Sugarman and Straus (1988) because fewer data are available on cities, and cities are inappropriate units of analysis for legal variables derived from state-level law. Because of restrictions inherent in the data, only two elements of gender equality—economic and social—were included in the analysis, even though the concept of gender equality and gender systems is much more complex.

The goal in determining economic equality for women was to find indicators that would measure women's status relative to men's, women's occupational prestige, and women's economic opportunity (or lack of it). Several indicators were included. With regard to relative status, wages and employment were the focus. Women's median income was computed as a percentage of men's median income to create the women's gender equality in income variable. Women's rates of employment were computed as a percentage of men's employment rates to create a measure of gender equality in employment. The percentage of women in managerial and technical professions was included as a measure of women's participation in nontraditional occupations. Women's employment rate and the percentage of single, female-headed households with children classified as poor were included as opportunity variables. These variables were taken from the census.

Social equality was more challenging. No direct measures of cultural beliefs and practices exist with regard to traditional gender roles and expectations, and no other studies have incorporated such measures. Thus social equality measures needed to be created, which required examining this social dimension of gender equality through the products of such belief and normative systems, as they are observable. The census provides little assistance in this regard, and other sources for such data at the city level are not available.

Two key areas of inequality in gender roles and expectations are marriage and the family. The census does track gender and marital status and heads of households and records the relationships of persons living in households. Through calculation, three measures were drawn from available census data. First, one would expect that in a highly traditional social gender system, few couples would report themselves as cohabiting. Nontraditional places would be characterized by both a higher rate of cohabitation and a willingness to report such relationships. Cohabitation reflects a lack of constraint by expectations for traditional marriage. Furthermore, cohabitation by gay and lesbian couples was included in the calculation, which reflects open acknowledgment of these nontraditional partner relationships.

An additional indicator of traditional expectations of marriage is reflected in the numbers of women who are separated or divorced. Strong marriage expectations can serve as a deterrent to divorce and can also be an incentive for those who are divorced to remarry. To represent the concept of how strong these expectations for marriage are for women, a measure was created from the numbers of women divorced or separated as a percentage of all women divorced or separated. As this measure focuses on women only, it is theorized to reflect women's willingness to live outside a marital relationship.

This divorce or separation measure differs from the overall measure of those divorced or separated in that it only examines women's lives. Additionally, this measure is not a pure mirror image of the overall percentage of those divorced and separated, as it is composed of those living with the status divorced or separated and does not indicate the rate at which marriages dissolve. Thus the percentage of those divorced or separated is high not only when women are leaving marriages but when they are staying out of them as well. Men may remarry at a different rate and represent a different proportion of divorced and separated persons than women do. Therefore the overall percentage of those divorced and separated is a more complete measure of unmarried persons and because it includes men is more of a measure of familial disruption. The percentage of women who are divorced or separated is interpreted differently from the overall measure, which is why it is included as a social equality variable. It represents the degree to which women are not following traditional expectations of being married. The likelihood of multicollinearity still exists, however, so interpretations of these variables constitute a crude exploration of the role women's divorce plays in women's homicide offending.

Finally, gender expectations play a large role in the division of child-rearing responsibilities. Unfortunately, no direct measure was available of the time men spent with their children compared with women's time with children. The census does give a breakdown of heads of household by marital status, gender, and presence of children, so it was possible to create a proxy for men's caring for children by examining the percentages of men who were single heads of households with children. As more men head households with children as single parents, the more we can argue that men and women come closer to having similar expectations for parenting and child rearing. Admittedly, this measure only approximates the gender distribution of child care and includes no measure of what occurs within two-parent families. The measure of how many single fathers are taking care of children, however, can give some indication of the social gender system with regard to who cares for children.

## Control Variables

For all analyses it was important to control for both population size and the percentage of the population (male or female) ages 15–39. Population size is important because different dynamics are at play within the largest cities than in smaller cities, and those dynamics need to be accounted for. The percentage of the population ages 15–39 is an important control for age structure. Youth have been shown to be more likely to engage in violence, and large numbers of youth may thus artificially contribute to higher rates of homicide. Both variables were derived from the census.

## Men's and Women's
## Homicide Offending: Descriptive Statistics

### Urban Homicide Statistics, General

Homicides in large cities comprised the majority of homicides in the United States during 1990. Of 23,440 homicides known to police in 1990, 13,927 occurred in cities with populations over 100,000.[3] This amounts to 59.4 percent of all homicides for the year. Cities ranged from no homicides (for example, Irvine, California) to 2,245 homicides (New York City).

Homicides in the 177 cities that participated in the SHR for 1990 were primarily committed by men. Of the 13,296 murders for which the gender of the offender was known, only 1,220 were committed by women. This constitutes 9.2 percent of all homicides in the represented cities—a finding consistent with other studies.

### Victim-Offender Relationships:
### Comparing Men and Women

Urban homicides most commonly occur among those who know each other. When the data are broken down by victim-offender relationship, 9,501 of the 13,296 homicides reported by the SHR involved a perpetrator and a victim who knew each other in some way. This constitutes 71.5 percent of all homicides for the 177 cities with populations over 100,000 who reported to the SHR. Broken down further, homicides involving acquaintances constituted 51 percent of all homicides in these cities, homicides involving family members accounted for 8.1 percent, and homicides involving intimate partners comprised 12.3 percent of all cases of homicide that were able to be classified (see Table 3.1).

Not surprisingly, the data show that men's homicides broken down by victim-offender relationship show similar patterns overall. What is interesting is the comparison of the patterns of victim-offender relationship for men's and women's homicide offending, as shown in Tables 3.2 and 3.3.

Stranger homicide, defined by a lack of prior relationship between offender and victim, had the greatest gender disparity in numbers. Men committed 3,711 stranger homicides in 1990, whereas women were responsible for only 84, according to the SHR. Thus of a total of 3,795 stranger homicides in 1990 in these large cities, 2.2 percent were perpetrated by women. The difference in rates is even more striking. In 1990 men committed 11.93 stranger homicides for

**Table 3.1    Total Urban Homicides by Victim-Offender Relationship, 1990**

| Victim-Offender Relationship | Homicides for 1990 | Percentage of Total | Homicide Rate |
|---|---|---|---|
| Stranger | 3,795 | 28.5 | 5.89 |
| Acquaintance | 6,775 | 51.0 | 10.51 |
| Family member | 1,085 | 8.1 | 1.68 |
| Partner | 1,641 | 12.3 | 2.54 |
| Total | 13,296[a] | 100.0 | 20.62 |

*Note:* a. This total reflects homicides reported in the SHR for which the gender of the offender was known.

**Table 3.2    Total Urban Homicides for Men by Victim-Offender Relationship, 1990**

| Victim-Offender Relationship | Men's Homicides | Percentage of Men's Total | Men's Rate | Men's Percentage of Victim-Offender Total |
|---|---|---|---|---|
| Stranger | 3,711 | 30.7 | 11.93 | 97.8 |
| Acquaintance | 6,340 | 52.5 | 20.39 | 93.6 |
| Family member | 864 | 7.2 | 2.77 | 79.6 |
| Partner | 1,161 | 9.6 | 3.73 | 70.7 |
| Total | 12,076 | 100.0 | 38.82 | 90.8 |

**Table 3.3    Total Urban Homicides for Women by Victim-Offender Relationship, 1990**

| Victim-Offender Relationship | Women's Homicides | Percentage of Women's Total | Women's Rate | Women's Percentage of Victim-Offender Total |
|---|---|---|---|---|
| Stranger | 84 | 6.9 | 0.25 | 2.2 |
| Acquaintance | 435 | 35.7 | 1.30 | 6.4 |
| Family member | 221 | 18.1 | 0.66 | 20.4 |
| Partner | 480 | 39.3 | 1.44 | 29.3 |
| Total | 1,220 | 100.0 | 3.65 | 9.2 |

every 100,000 men in the cities. For every 100,000 women, 0.25 homicides were committed by women. Continuity is seen between these findings and other studies that report the number of stranger homicides to be much larger for men.

With increased familiarity between victim and offender, the gender gap begins to close. Acquaintance homicides by women totaled 435, 6.4 percent of the 6,775 total acquaintance homicides. Although this figure still falls far short of parity between men's and women's homicide offending, it is a smaller gap than that with stranger homicide and is even smaller than the 9.2 percent representation of women in total homicides. The gap in rates, however, is very large. For every 100,000 men, 20.39 acquaintance homicide offenses were committed by men. For every 100,000 women, 1.3 were committed by women. Acquaintance homicide offending is still much more prevalent for men.

Homicides involving family members and intimate partners show the smallest gender gaps. Women's family homicides comprised 221 of a total of 1,085 family homicides, or 20.4 percent, a greater number than women's representation in overall homicides. The family rate for women was lower than that of acquaintances, but the gap between men and women in rates of family killing was much smaller (2.77 versus 0.66). The gender gap in homicide offending for 1990 was smallest for homicide of intimate partners. Of 1,641 homicides of intimate partners, 29.3 percent (480) were attributed to women—again a higher number than their representation but not close to parity.

Thus urban homicide is committed predominantly by males at all levels. The closer the relationship between victim and offender, the greater the representation of women. Women and men, however, never reach complete parity in homicides in any category.

## Victim-Offender Relationships: Comparing Homicides Within Gender

Women and men also differ in the distribution of homicides over victim-offender relationship categories. In 1990 homicides in large cities, men who killed most frequently killed acquaintances (52.5 percent). Second among men's homicide victims were strangers, who accounted for 30.7 percent of men's homicide incidences. From other research one would expect a fairly large proportion of these cases to be felony related, but the data available for this analysis did not allow for an exact breakdown. Family members (at 7.2 percent) and intimate partners (at 9.6 percent) were less frequent victims, even combined.

Women, on the other hand, most often killed intimate partners when they did kill. In the 1990 sample 39.3 percent of all women's homicides involved an intimate partner (480 of 1,220 women's homicides). Next most prevalent were 435 acquaintance homicides, which constituted 35.7 percent of women's homicide cases. Family homicide made up 18.1 percent (221 cases). Stranger homicide was the least frequent type for women, constituting only 6.9 percent of homicides perpetrated by women in the cities represented in the SHR.

In addition to the gender gap in women's homicide offending, a distinctly different picture of patterns of men's and women's homicide offending is revealed by these data. Men kill strangers much more often than women do. Women are more likely than men to kill intimate partners when they choose to kill. Although acquaintances were frequent victims of both men and women, their predominance as men's victims was unmatched by women killers.

Overall, the majority of U.S. homicides occur in the largest cities. Women represented less than 10 percent of homicide offenders in those cities. The SHR data revealed that the majority of homicides in those cities in 1990 involved acquaintances and strangers. This pattern, however, reflected men's homicide. Women, in contrast, most often killed intimate partners, followed by acquaintances. Men's victims tend to be killed in contexts associated with public space such as bar brawls, gang violence (e.g., drive-by shootings, fights over turf), lethal confrontations in such areas as workplaces, and in other felony-related contexts such as robberies. When women kill, the contexts tend to be in the private, domestic sphere and include intimate partners, children, and elders. These differing patterns encourage us to question theories that presume homicide is unaffected by gender and gender circumstances.

## Men's and Women's Homicide Offending: Analysis of Differences

There are two major descriptive differences between men's and women's homicide—the volume of overall homicide offending and the distribution of homicides by victim-offender relationship. Traditional homicide theory has failed to consider the impact of these differences, which has resulted in a dual weakness in homicide studies to date. First, because differences in gendered experiences are ignored theoretically, research has failed to disaggregate homicide by gender, resulting in conclusions about homicide that may be flawed or weakened because such differences are not made visible and accounted for. Second, criminology is denied important analysis of women's homicide, without which it is unable to see the applicability of traditional homicide theory to women and how this differs from its usefulness for men. Also, even though women constitute a small number of offenders overall, the act of homicide is serious enough to try to explain all offending, not just the roughly 90 percent attributable to men. Additionally, to discount women ignores the value of women's lives and experiences and minimizes their importance in understanding the contexts that produce lethal violence by women. Attention to these issues can help in the prevention of homicides by women offenders.

To address how well current homicide variables explain women's offending, we need to examine men's and women's homicide offending rates using traditional predictors of homicide.[4] Regression analysis is done for the total (aggregated) rate and for intimate partner, family, and acquaintance rates of homicide. We can examine the generalizability question with a look at three portions of the analysis. One consideration is whether differences between the individual coefficients in the two models are significant. In other words, do the variables operate in a statistically similar way in explaining women's versus men's homicide offending? A t-test was conducted to test whether the difference between the women's and men's individual coefficients for the variables was significant. Another consideration is the direction of variables that differ significantly. Even if a variable is significant for both men and women, if the direction of the effects is opposite we can question the generalizability of the predictor. Clearly, if a variable significantly increases men's homicide offending but significantly decreases that for women, the variable cannot be operating similarly for both. This also holds if the significant variables are in a direction contrary to the theoretical prediction.

Finally, it is possible to assess whether the traditional model equally explains men's and women's homicide offending through a comparison of variance explained ($R^2$), which measures the overall success of the variables in the model. If a difference is found in the variance explained for men's and women's homicide offending, the models do not work equally by gender. The larger the difference, the less they are generalizable.[5]

### Total Homicide Rates by Gender

Ordinary least squares (OLS) multiple regression and seemingly unrelated regression (SURE) were first conducted with 1990 men's and women's total homicide rates as the dependent variables (see Table 3.4). The variables drawn from social disorganizational theory were somewhat successful in the whole equation analyzing men's homicide rates. Although population change did not impact men's homicide offending, population density, percentage of those divorced or separated, and percentage of African Americans were all positive and significant. This means that as crowding in cities, familial instability, and racial heterogeneity increased, men's homicide offending rates significantly increased overall. Thus there is evidence that ecological factors do play a role in creating an environment for men's overall lethal violence.

This was less the case for overall women's homicide offending. The social disorganizational predictors did not fare equally as well in explaining women's rates. Population change was insignificant, as

**Table 3.4   Men's and Women's Total Homicide Rates**

| Variable | Men's | | | Women's | | | Difference of Coefficient | |
|---|---|---|---|---|---|---|---|---|
| | b | Beta | p | b | Beta | p | t | p |
| Percentage of families in poverty | 0.059 | 0.366 | <0.001 | 0.042 | 0.292 | <0.001 | –3.375 | <0.001 |
| Log of population density | 0.254 | 0.185 | 0.002 | –0.169 | –0.140 | 0.045 | –5.281 | <0.001 |
| Log of percentage change | 0.466 | 0.084 | 0.128 | –0.358 | –0.073 | 0.270 | 0.631 | 0.530 |
| Percentage divorced or separated | 0.083 | 0.179 | 0.002 | 0.084 | 0.207 | 0.003 | –0.905 | 0.367 |
| Log of percentage African American | 0.282 | 0.381 | <0.001 | 0.172 | 0.263 | 0.001 | –3.027 | 0.002 |
| Confederate South | 0.285 | 0.130 | 0.018 | 0.222 | 0.115 | 0.082 | 0.710 | 0.479 |
| Population total | <0.001 | 0.087 | 0.065 | <0.001 | 0.091 | 0.110 | –2.140 | 0.032 |
| Log of percentage 15–39 | –0.372 | –0.031 | 0.533 | –0.049 | –0.005 | 0.937 | –0.872 | 0.385 |
| Adjusted $R^2$ | | 0.657 | | | 0.499 | | — | |
| Significance of F | | <0.001 | | | <0.001 | | — | |

we saw in the men's analysis. Percentage of those divorced or separated and percentage of African Americans were both positively and significantly related to women's homicide offending, meaning familial instability and racial heterogeneity significantly increased the rate at which women killed. The effect of the percentage of African Americans was, however, significantly different and stronger in the men's equation than in the women's. Therefore although racial heterogeneity has a positive effect on the rate of women's homicide, it is not as strong a factor for women as it is for men.

Population density, as in the men's analysis, was a significant factor for women's homicide offending rates. Unlike the men's equations, population density is significant in the opposite direction than was observed for men and is predicted by social disorganizational theory. That is, whereas one would expect to see an increase in women's homicide offending as population density increases, the converse occurs. The fewer the number of persons per square mile, the higher the women's homicide offending rate. The difference between the two equations for population density was also significant. Thus although crowded cities were significant in predicting men's homicide, women's homicide offending rates were significantly higher the less crowded the cities were.

The variable measuring economic deprivation—percentage of families in poverty—significantly increased both men's and women's homicide offending rates. Thus poverty provides conditions in which men and women overall will commit more lethal violence. Whereas the impact of poverty was important for understanding men's and women's homicide offending, the impact of poverty for men was significantly stronger, meaning it was even more important for understanding men's homicide offending.

The effect of being in the South appeared different for men and women on the surface. Cities in the Confederate South had a significantly higher rate of men's homicide than cities in the North, although the rates of overall women's homicide were not significantly different. Thus assuming we accept the subculture of violence argument, men in the South live under a normative acceptance of violence, but that does not appear to operate in the same way for women. When the difference in coefficients was examined, however, there were no significant differences between the two. Thus although the South achieves significance for men, it operates in essentially the same way for men and women.

The variables of age structure and population size were not important factors for either equation. The control variables of population size and percentage of those ages 15–39 did not differ between the men's and women's equations. Neither control variable achieved significance for women. The difference between coefficients for the percentage ages 15–39 was insignificant, and population size was significantly different between the two equations, although it was insignificant for both.

With regard to overall homicide offending rates, variables drawn from traditional theories differ somewhat in their ability to explain men's and women's homicide offending. Although poverty, family instability, and racial heterogeneity significantly increase both men's and women's homicide offending, poverty and racial heterogeneity are significantly stronger factors for men than for women. This finding raises questions of generalizability, even though the effects are significant for both. Population change and percentage of youth are not significant for either men's or women's rates, nor do they differ significantly between them. Although population size was insignificant for both, it did differ significantly in its impact, with men's homicide offending affected more by population size. The South indicator, although significant only for men, did not differ significantly from its effect on women's homicide offending.

The impact of crowding, seen in population density, shows a major divergence between the men's and women's equations, which raises questions about whether traditional theory is equally usable for understanding women. The effect of population density on women's homicide offending challenges traditional theoretical thinking about homicide as seen in the men's analysis. Existing theory would predict that crowding would increase women's rate of killing, but instead we discover a significant and opposite finding. Thus crowding in cities has a very different effect on women than it does on men, and there is a high statistical significance to that difference.

Finally, there is evidence for limitations in the generalizability of traditional homicide theory in the amount of variance explained between men's and women's homicides. A substantial difference in the amount of the homicide rate is explained between the two analyses. The traditional predictors were 65.7 percent successful in explaining the variance in men's homicide rates but only 49.9 percent successful for women's. Thus the complete model was less successful for explaining women's overall homicide than it was for men's.

Comparing men's and women's overall homicide offending rates is only the beginning. Important information is lost when one considers only overall rates. As Kirk Williams and Robert Flewelling (1988) demonstrated, homicide offending rates and their predictors differ when the relationship between victim and offender is considered, showing that factors influence the use of lethal violence differently depending on the context in which the killing takes place. Thus any test of traditional theoretical generalizability must examine types of homicide and the usefulness of commonly used predictors against gender-specific homicide data.

The context represented by different relationships reflects very different acts. The biggest difference comes from the public–private sphere distinction. Most family member and intimate partner killings occur in the home. Influences such as a culture of violence or loss of community control may have a lesser effect on such homicides than they do on acquaintance or stranger homicide. Moreover, the general image of homicide and violence, both in the public's impression and reflected in theory, is that which occurs in the public sphere, such as between acquaintances and strangers (see Gillespie, 1989, for a discussion of this assumption in self-defense law). As feminist research has shown, men and women have very different kinds of lives within the public and private spheres, including differences in the amounts of time spent in each. Gender disparities will likely be seen within these contexts and perhaps will have patterns distinct from the overall analyses.

### Intimate Partner Homicide Rates by Gender

The most common image of homicides, as just discussed, is of a public crime involving gang shootings, fights, and strangers jumping from bushes to rob and kill victims. The homicide of intimate partners, then, is outside that "typical" image. The homicide of intimate partners seems inconsistent with the predominant view of homicide as involving strangers or acquaintances, since theory has evolved around presumptions of men not only as perpetrators but as perpetrators against nonintimates. Traditional models of homicide may be less useful for this kind of homicide. OLS regression and SURE were used to analyze men's and women's intimate partner homicide offending rates using traditional predictors. As one could expect and as Table 3.5 reveals, the pattern of explanation by the variables is different in some ways than was seen in the analysis of overall homicide rates.

The most striking and surprising observation is that the traditionally derived predictors, on the surface, seem to better predict women's intimate partner homicide. These traditional models were based more on men's public spheres, so we would expect that men's and women's intimate partner homicide offending would be less well explained overall and that women's intimate partner offending would be explained less, not more, than men's. The only predictor with any significant effect in the men's intimate partner homicide equation was the percentage of African Americans, which significantly increased the rate at which men killed intimate partners. None of the other social disorganizational variables made a significant impact, nor did poverty, the South, or the control variables. This stands in sharp contrast to the analysis of men's overall homicide in which the traditional variables did a better job of explaining men's homicide.

More predictors were significant in explaining women's intimate partner homicide than were significant for men. The social disorgani-

**Table 3.5   Men's and Women's Intimate Partner Homicide Rates**

| Variable | Men's | | | Women's | | | Difference of Coefficient | |
|---|---|---|---|---|---|---|---|---|
| | b | Beta | p | b | Beta | p | t | p |
| Percentage of families in poverty | 0.019 | 0.142 | 0.118 | 0.028 | 0.249 | 0.004 | –0.573 | 0.568 |
| Log of population density | 0.061 | 0.055 | 0.520 | –0.141 | –0.152 | 0.063 | 3.070 | 0.002 |
| Log of percentage change | –0.013 | –0.003 | 0.972 | 0.059 | 0.016 | 0.840 | 0.914 | 0.362 |
| Percentage divorced or separated | 0.058 | 0.154 | 0.064 | 0.050 | 0.159 | 0.045 | –0.233 | 0.816 |
| Log of percentage African American | 0.167 | 0.277 | 0.003 | 0.110 | 0.218 | 0.014 | –1.219 | 0.224 |
| Confederate South | 0.042 | 0.024 | 0.771 | 0.115 | 0.077 | 0.319 | 1.409 | 0.160 |
| Population total | <0.001 | 0.105 | 0.129 | <0.001 | 0.038 | 0.564 | –1.903 | 0.057 |
| Log of percentage 15–39 | –0.945 | –0.098 | 0.186 | –1.137 | –0.141 | 0.048 | –0.696 | 0.488 |
| Adjusted $R^2$ | | 0.253 | | | 0.318 | | — | |
| Significance of F | | <0.001 | | | <0.001 | | — | |

zational variables were reasonably successful in explaining women's intimate partner homicide. As would be predicted, increases in the percentage of those divorced or separated and of African Americans resulted in increased women's intimate partner rates. Contrary to social disorganizational predictions, population density was negatively related to women's intimate partner rates. The coefficient for this variable approached statistical significance. Thus as cities became less congested, women's intimate partner homicide offending became more frequent, not less frequent as would be predicted. Poverty also had a significant and positive impact on women's intimate partner homicide offending. In other words, the greater the poverty in a city, the higher the rate at which women killed intimate partners. The finding that a higher percentage of those ages 15–39 decreased women's intimate partner homicide rates was contrary to prediction. Traditionally, the greater the number of youth, the more homicide is predicted. In this case, however, a greater proportion of young people actually decreased women's killing of intimate partners.

Despite the dissimilar patterns of significance of the variables between men's and women's intimate partner homicide offending, t-tests revealed that overall, the coefficients did not differ significantly from each other between men's and women's intimate partner homicide analyses. This means that although more factors were significant for both women and men, the predictors worked in the same ways and were not fundamentally different. The only exception was population density, which was insignificant for both genders but showed a significantly different effect between men's and women's intimate partner homicide offending. The negative relationship observed for women with regard to population density clearly questions the utility of this theorizing for women who kill intimate partners. These observations need to be taken with some caution, however, as the ability to create constructs from secondary data is limited, and there are not precise measures that fully reflect our theories.

The analysis of intimate partner homicide rates provides several points of interest for generalizability. First, the traditional predictors of homicide appear to better predict women's than men's intimate partner homicide rates, which means they are less applicable for men's partner homicide than for women's. The utility of the indicators, however, does not necessarily mean the theory is useful in its original form. This is indicated in the social disorganization variables. Whereas heterogeneity and familial instability act in the predicted ways to increase intimate partner killing, the fact that population density nearly significantly decreased women's intimate partner homicide offending points to an alternative view of social disorganization and the killing of women's intimate partners. Instead of a focus on a highly dense urban population and the theory that women exhibit low informal social control, a different angle emerges from this analysis. Areas with fewer persons per square mile may allow relatively more privacy and, for some, more possibilities for isolation from others. This may be reflected in more single-family dwellings with yard space and fewer congested apartment complexes and houses with little room between them. The more space there is, the less neighbors can hear conflict, and the less interaction with fellow residents is required. These conditions can help domestic violence to thrive.

A racially heterogeneous environment may add to the problem because there may not be a strong cultural community to lend support or encourage activity that would take a woman outside the home. This is intensified by familial instability, which shifts focus away from participation in the community and toward internal family matters. Isolation has been found to be linked to battering (e.g., Nielson, Endo, and Ellington, 1992) and to women's intimate killings (e.g., Browne, 1987; Totman, 1978). Thus disorganization could have this particular impact on women. Overall, however, men do not seem to be affected by most of the traditional factors in their killing of intimate partners and need their own analytical and theoretical development.

A second important aspect of these results involves the low success rate of the overall models for men and women in explaining the rates of killing intimates. The model including the traditional variables explained only 31.8 percent of the variance in women's intimate partner homicide rates and 25.3 percent of men's intimate partner homicide rates. There is a 6.5 percent better success rate in modeling women's intimate partner offending rates, though both $R^2$ scores are quite low. This difference in the women's and men's analyses cannot be attributed to a lower number of men's intimate partner homicides, which were more than double those of women.

One source of difficulty may be the lack of precise indicators of the theories. From this analysis, traditional theories of homicide do not appear to explain intimate partner homicide very well for either gender, and we need to explore further these and alternative explanations. Clearly, the involvement of domestic violence in such homicides requires consideration of gender and gender inequalities, something traditional theories do not include. Additionally, the fact that overall the variable coefficients from the regression models were not significantly different from each other suggests that men's and women's homicide offending rates for intimate partners are affected in much the same way by the traditional predictors, thus making the predictors generalizable to women. Given the poor performance of the models for both, however, we can conclude that traditional models are lacking—albeit equally—for explaining both men's and women's intimate partner homicide offending. The exclusion of gender considerations in traditional theorizing and the possibility of common factors that may underlie both men's and women's killing of intimate partners (such as domestic violence) need more examination.

## Family Homicide Rates by Gender

Another type of homicide is that between family members. The comparability of traditional theories in explaining family homicide by male and female perpetrators was examined. Men's and women's family homicide offending rates were analyzed using traditional predictors using OLS regression and SURE (see Table 3.6). Like the case of intimate homicide offenders, the vision is not usually one of parents, siblings, and other relatives killing each other. For this reason, traditional theory would be expected to be less strong in explaining this type of homicide as well. As expected, family homicide was also poorly explained by traditional predictors for either gender.

Both men's and women's family homicide rates were impacted by the percentage of those divorced and separated, which significantly increased the rate at which both men and women killed family members. This shows that family instability has a similar tendency to increase the risk of lethal violence against nonintimate family members regardless of the offender's gender. The effect of family instability, however, was significantly different and thus was stronger for men's family offending. Although the effects for both genders were significant, this predictor had a more important impact on men's lethal violence against family members.

**Table 3.6   Men's and Women's Family Homicide Rates**

| Variable | Men's | | | Women's | | | Difference of Coefficient | |
|---|---|---|---|---|---|---|---|---|
| | b | Beta | p | b | Beta | p | t | p |
| Percentage of families in poverty | 0.034 | 0.264 | 0.002 | 0.013 | 0.162 | 0.081 | −4.190 | <0.001 |
| Log of population density | −0.040 | 0.037 | 0.630 | −0.013 | −0.020 | 0.822 | −0.410 | 0.683 |
| Log of percentage change | −0.158 | −0.036 | 0.622 | −0.034 | −0.012 | 0.882 | 2.870 | 0.004 |
| Percentage divorced or separated | 0.079 | 0.218 | 0.004 | 0.056 | 0.245 | 0.004 | −3.246 | 0.001 |
| Log of percentage African American | 0.086 | 0.148 | 0.079 | 0.043 | 0.119 | 0.211 | −3.356 | <0.001 |
| Confederate South | 0.113 | 0.066 | 0.370 | 0.110 | 0.102 | 0.218 | −0.693 | 0.490 |
| Population total | <0.001 | 0.168 | 0.008 | <0.001 | 0.068 | 0.339 | −2.498 | 0.012 |
| Log of percentage 15–39 | −1.473 | −0.158 | 0.020 | −0.479 | −0.082 | 0.281 | 2.459 | 0.014 |
| Adjusted $R^2$ | | 0.386 | | | 0.215 | | | — |
| Significance of F | | <0.001 | | | <0.001 | | | — |

Poverty and population size significantly increased the rate of family homicides by men, as predicted by traditional theory, but neither had a significant effect for women. Significant differences were found in the coefficients for men for these variables compared with women's coefficients, meaning they are indeed factors that increase men's family killing but not women's. The percentage of the population ages 15–39 actually decreased the rate of men's family killing—contrary to prediction—but had no significant impact on women's family homicide rates. This is another variable that differs significantly from its women's counterpart. Perhaps the age of risk for men's lethal violence toward family members is higher than for other kinds of homicide. Youth homicide is not generally characterized by family killing. Possible effects of younger populations and changing values toward child discipline may also be at work. The empirical evidence remains that traditional notions of a younger population as a greater risk for lethal violence do not hold in the case of men's family homicide.

Two other coefficients, although insignificant for both men's and women's family killing, showed significant differences that raise questions about the equal applicability of traditional homicide theory to homicides by gender: the percentage of African Americans, insignificant but positive for both, and population change, insignificantly positive for women and negative for men. Although the substantive contributions of these variables are not noteworthy, the significant differences between them add to the questioning of generalizability.

Overall, both different patterns of significance and significant differences between coefficients raised questions about the equal applicability of traditional predictors to men's and women's family homicide offending.

What is particularly notable in this analysis is the low amount of success for the traditional variables when applied to rates of killing for both men and women. Traditional predictors better explained family homicide offending for men than for women, which indicates that the gender bias in the theory is generally working against women, even when it comes to rates of family killing. The variance for explaining men's and women's family homicide differed by 17.1 percent. $R^2$, however, was quite low for both equations—0.386 for men and 0.215 for women. Traditional predictors are clearly poor explanations for women's family homicide rates, and although they do better for men's rates, they do not explain them very well. Again, this indicates that not only is the traditional theorizing about homicide inadequate for explaining women's rates of killing family members but that something about familial relations not captured by non-gendered theories is a more important key to understanding the rates at which women and men kill family members.

## Acquaintance Homicide Rates by Gender

When men's and women's acquaintance homicides are compared, an interesting phenomenon emerges. First, we know much more about women's homicides in more private relationships, like those with family members and intimate partners. The notion of acquaintance homicide brings to mind images of conflicts outside the home and a picture much closer to that embodied in theories about culture and macrolevel structures. As such, acquaintance homicide rates may be less likely to show significant divergence between men and women. The image of homicide between acquaintances is one that is more public and that occurs between persons with less binding and more voluntary relationships. Thus many of the differences between men's and women's lives may be less prominent in homicide offending of this type.

Comparisons were made in men's and women's acquaintance homicide rates through OLS and SURE regression analysis using the traditional predictors, as depicted in Table 3.7. The analysis shows points of similarity and difference between men's and women's acquaintance homicide rates, at least on the surface. In general, the traditional predictors were only partially useful in predicting acquaintance homicides by both men and women. Poverty increased acquaintance homicide rates significantly for both men and women, although the coefficient for men was significantly different and stronger. Thus although structural poverty had an important impact on increasing the rates of acquaintance killing for both men and women, it was more important for understanding men's rates.

Similarly, cities in the South were characterized by higher acquaintance homicide rates for both men and women, suggesting that the influence of being in the South is generally the same for men and women regarding acquaintances. From the argument of the subculture of violence theory, this would imply that men and women are fairly equally affected by an environment that is more likely to

**Table 3.7    Men's and Women's Acquaintance Homicide Rates**

| Variable | Men's | | | Women's | | | Difference of Coefficient | |
|---|---|---|---|---|---|---|---|---|
| | b | Beta | p | b | Beta | p | t | p |
| Percentage of families in poverty | 0.060 | 0.334 | <0.001 | 0.021 | 0.198 | 0.020 | –7.123 | <0.001 |
| Log of population density | 0.201 | 0.132 | 0.042 | –0.026 | –0.029 | 0.713 | –2.706 | 0.007 |
| Log of percentage change | 0.289 | 0.047 | 0.446 | –0.612 | –0.172 | 0.024 | 3.079 | 0.002 |
| Percentage divorced or separated | 0.056 | 0.108 | 0.085 | 0.061 | 0.205 | 0.009 | –4.132 | <0.001 |
| Log of percentage African American | 0.316 | 0.383 | <0.001 | 0.058 | 0.122 | 0.159 | –7.181 | <0.001 |
| Confederate South | 0.409 | 0.168 | 0.007 | 0.294 | 0.210 | 0.006 | –1.778 | 0.075 |
| Population total | <0.001 | 0.071 | 0.176 | <0.001 | 0.103 | 0.114 | –2.392 | 0.016 |
| Log of percentage 15–39 | –0.867 | –0.066 | 0.242 | 1.144 | 0.151 | 0.031 | 2.192 | 0.028 |
| Adjusted $R^2$ | | 0.572 | | | 0.348 | | | — |
| Significance of F | | <0.001 | | | <0.001 | | | — |

accept violence. Because poverty and other possible confounding influences are taken into account, this theorized cultural influence in the South may make men and women more likely overall to resort to lethal violence against acquaintances. This is further supported by a lack of significant difference between the coefficients. Population size was insignificant for both men's and women's acquaintance killing, although the coefficients were significantly different.

Several indicators showed different patterns of significance between men's and women's acquaintance killing. Population density significantly increased men's acquaintance killing, whereas it had an insignificant effect on women's acquaintance offending rates. This means not only that city crowding is an important factor in increasing men's killing of acquaintances but that women do not experience it in the same way. The significant difference between these coefficients only underscores that this variable is not applicable to women's rates of acquaintance killing. The percentage of those ages 15–39 significantly increased women's acquaintance homicide offending rates, as predicted by traditional theory, although it had an insignificant effect on men's rates. The difference between these coefficients was also significant. This finding indicates that in this analysis, age composition may be a traditional factor that has more applicability to women's acquaintance homicide than it does for men's.

The percentage of those divorced and separated significantly increased women's rate of killing acquaintances, as would be predicted, but had no effect on the men's rate. The difference in these coefficients was significant. Again, as was seen in age composition, in this area traditional theory may be more applicable to women's acquaintance homicides than to those of men. The percentage of African Americans significantly increased the men's acquaintance homicide rate, as predicted, but not the women's rate. Coefficient differences were significant as well. In this case traditional thinking about heterogeneity clearly does not apply to women's acquaintance homicide offending as it does for men's. Contrary to traditional predictions, a greater percentage of change in the population between 1980 and 1990 significantly *decreased* the women's homicide rate, with a coefficient that significantly differed from the men's. Although some unmeasured characteristics of these cities likely contributed to decreased women's lethal violence against acquaintances, this finding contradicts social disorganization's prediction that population turnover increases homicide.

Overall, the analyses show that applying standard indicators of traditional theory to men's and women's acquaintance homicide results in more dissimilar than similar findings. Differences are found in the social disorganizational variables of population change, percentage of African Americans, population density, and percentage of those divorced or separated—suggesting that social disorganization and its effects on acquaintance homicide do differ by gender, even though similarities exist between men and women in acquaintance homicide. Additionally, differences in the percentage of those ages 15–39 show that the younger the population, the greater the women's acquaintance homicide rate. In addition to the patterns of difference in significance are the supporting findings that all of the variables, except the South, differ significantly between men's and women's equations.

When the overall success of traditional predictors and explaining acquaintance homicide by gender is examined, traditional predictors have greater success in explaining both men's and women's acquaintance homicide rates than for any other victim-offender relationship. The amount of men's acquaintance homicide offending explained by the model is good. Of the variance in men's acquaintance homicide, 57.2 percent is explained using traditional homicide variables. Although 34.8 percent of women's acquaintance homicide explained is also relatively good, a very large difference is found in the usefulness of traditional homicide models by gender; in terms of statistical variance explained, the predictors explained 22.4 percent more variance when applied to men's acquaintance killing compared with that of women. Thus the model as a whole was not equally successful for men's and women's rates of acquaintance killing, lending support to questions of the theory that men and women kill under similar overall conditions, although acquaintance homicide would appear to be the type of homicide that would most likely be similar between men and women.

Overall, the analysis of traditional homicide explanations for men's and women's homicide offending rates shows differences in the effectiveness of traditionally used variables. This held for analyses using overall homicide rates and, in general, for rates broken down into three categories of victim-offender relationships: intimate partner, family, and acquaintance. For three of the four analyses, traditional models are less successful in explaining women's homicide than men's as measured by patterns of significance, significance in coefficient differences, and overall variance explained. This is highly supportive of the contention that traditional homicide theory is not gender-neutral and that in fact it is a better reflection of the factors affecting men who kill.

There was one exception to the finding that traditional homicide theory is not gender-neutral. For intimate partner homicide, the traditional predictors fared better for women than for men, and maximum likelihood analysis showed that the predictors were operating in insignificantly different ways. The finding that for women, population density operates in the opposite direction of that predicted, however, does pose a challenge to the applicability of traditional theory to women's homicide offending rates. This is particularly important given what is known qualitatively about women's killing of intimate partners. The connection between domestic abuse, self-defensive killing, and the isolation of the abusive household cannot be overlooked. In this case the lack of density of a city's population may provide a greater barrier to assistance and community support that could help abused women before lethal violence results. Contrast this with the traditional (and possibly male-centered) interpretation of density as causing increased psychosocial stress, resulting in increased irritation and anger. Although most of the predictors worked similarly, the case of population density clearly calls traditional explanations of homicide into question when they pertain to intimate partner killing as well.

The relative similarities in the utility of traditional explanations for men and women in the killing of intimate partners are also indicative of another factor not included in the traditional models. The context of the killing of intimate partners for both men and women offenders is often that of domestic violence. A man's killing of his spouse or lover is linked to a history of abuse as often as a woman's self-defensive killing of her partner. Thus the equations are likely to respond similarly to the same factors because of the common factor of domestic abuse.

When men's intimate partner homicide is included with traditional predictors for women's intimate homicide rates (see Table 3.8), it is the single most significant factor in explaining women's killing of intimate partners. It is so significant that it weakens the impact of the other traditional variables and substantially increases the overall variance explained in the model. Thus the apparent success of some traditional predictors in explaining women's rates of intimate partner killing may result more from the fact that this killing is likely tied to men's violence against women and the impact these factors have on men. The effect of these variables on women's offending is not direct. This suggests a somewhat more complex

**Table 3.8  Traditional Homicide Predictors, Men's Intimate Partner Homicide, and Women's Intimate Homicide Rates**

| Variable | b | Beta | p |
|---|---|---|---|
| Log of percentage African American | <0.001 | 0.148 | 0.092 |
| Percentage of families in poverty | <0.001 | 0.206 | 0.014 |
| Log of percentage population change | 0.112 | 0.030 | 0.695 |
| Log of population density | –0.160 | –0.172 | 0.026 |
| Percentage of total population divorced or separated | <0.001 | 0.114 | 0.138 |
| Confederate South | 0.106 | 0.071 | 0.335 |
| Percentage female 15–39 | <0.001 | –0.126 | 0.069 |
| Population size (1990) | <0.001 | 0.008 | 0.895 |
| Log of men's intimate homicide | 0.238 | 0.283 | <0.001 |
| Adjusted $R^2$ | — | 0.376 | — |
| Significance of F | — | <0.001 | — |

model for women's intimate partner killing that incorporates violence against women as a more immediate factor through which many other variables operate.

An additional consideration in the interpretation of the results of the intimate partner homicide analysis is the relative overall lack of success of the indicators in explaining either men's or women's killing of intimate partners. This finding, in conjunction with the low explanatory power of traditional models for the killing of other family members, suggests that traditional homicide predictors are most useful in general for those homicide rates more likely to reflect general images of homicide as a more public and distant relational act, as we see in acquaintance killing. Therefore, in addition to the exclusion of gender in traditional modeling, there is an exclusion of private-sphere dynamics that are more likely to affect the killing of intimates and family members, whether by men or women. The fact that women have traditionally been the primary occupants of the household reinforces the fact that domestic homicide, "women's homicide," has generally been overlooked in traditional theories of homicide offending.

In conclusion, this study strongly shows that men and women are different in the volume of offending, in victim-offender patterns, and in factors that influence the rates of homicide offending. Furthermore, traditional models leave much to be desired in explaining women's homicide offending rates. Given the lack of variables that reflect women's relative position in these cities and the demonstrated importance of such factors as employment and social freedom in overall well-being, it is logical to explore the role gender plays in women's homicide offending.

## Notes

1. Comparison with 1990 UCR data revealed that 2 of the missing cities had no homicides in 1990, 12 cities reported homicides to the UCR but not to the SHR, and 9 cities had missing data in both. Several of the 12 cities that did not report to the SHR were in Florida, which because of reporting problems did not report to the SHR in 1990. The 2 cities that reported no homicides to the UCR—Scottsdale, Arizona, and Irvine, California—were recoded as zero for all categories of homicide incidences. The totals for the 12 cities that reported to the UCR were added to the city

total variable. Thus 179 cities were available for gender-specific analysis, and 191 cities were used for aggregated homicide summary statistics.

2. The use of the city as the unit of analysis in social disorganization theory is not entirely in keeping with the theory, although it is preferable to using higher levels of aggregation. As Robert Bursik (1988) states, the original unit of analysis in social disorganization theory was the neighborhood, and that is the appropriate level at which to test the theory. In homicide study, however, the neighborhood or census-tract level provides too few homicides for each included area. Thus rates cannot be calculated. Although use of the city as the unit of analysis does obscure those residential separations originally theorized, it has become an accepted unit of analysis for this kind of social disorganizational application. Additionally, one can argue that a city does share some characteristics of a community as well. For these reasons, the city is the best unit of analysis.

3. This total was obtained using SHR data for homicide totals, where available, and UCR numbers of homicides for cities with UCR data but no SHR data.

4. It is conceivable that men's and women's homicide offending rates will have some commonality, despite any observed differences. One such commonality is seen in correlated residuals. It is important to examine statistically the degree to which these findings have been influenced by correlated residuals that exert hidden influences in the direction of both equations. If residuals are highly correlated, unmeasured variables can be seen to confound observed predictors in equations. After correlated residuals are identified, it will be necessary to control for those common influences.

The exploration of unmeasured, common influences between the men's and women's equations begins with saving regression residuals and analyzing the correlation between those residuals for each type of homicide for men and women. For all types of homicide, the correlation between residuals in the two equations was moderate but significant. The majority of the correlations were between 0.2 and 0.3, which means some commonality in unexplained variance exists between the men's and women's equations. These common factors could drive the indicators toward more or less similarity, depending on the influence of the common factor. Because these correlations are fairly small, however, the influence of the unmeasured commonalities would also be small. The very low correlation of the family equation residuals, at 0.157, suggests a very low level of commonality in unexplained variance, which would have a very small influence, if any, on the predictors. Because we want the most precise statement possible about differences between predictors, further analysis to eliminate the impact of these correlated residuals is needed.

Seemingly unrelated regression analysis was done to examine regression results with correlated residuals taken into account. SURE estimates the two equations simultaneously as one large equation, so a maximum likelihood test for differences between coefficients controlling for correlated error was possible.

The results from the SURE analysis were identical to the OLS regression results. This occurs when the independent variables (and, subsequently, values on the predictors) are the same for both equations. Thus the regression coefficients and p values from the OLS analysis have not been influenced by the small amount of correlated error. The results reported, then, reflect both analyses (see Kennedy, 1996). Although SURE does not improve on OLS in this instance, SURE was done to allow us to perform the t-test described earlier.

5. The $R^2$ comparisons should be considered to be descriptive and be taken cautiously in the absence of a direct assessment of whether the difference in $R^2$ is significant.

# 4

## Gender Equality and Women's Homicide Rates

A lack of gender consideration in traditional homicide theory limits the ability to explain women's homicide offending. A feminist model of women's homicide offending rates can better explain the circumstances under which the majority of women kill. When gender equality is low, a lower presence of resources and opportunities exists for women to break free from abusive partners, traditional stresses of child rearing, and oppressed lives. With limited resources and simultaneous stresses as a result of patriarchal systems, women in areas of low gender equality are much more likely to be placed in situations where lethal violence is probable.

Gender equality is argued to best address homicide rates related to women's subordinate status within an unequal social system. Women's relative disadvantage in such a gender-unequal system involves a strong emphasis on women playing traditional roles in the home and a concurrent disadvantage in the public spheres of work and social freedom. As such, domestic homicide rates for women's offending should be better explained by conditions of low gender equality. Explaining acquaintance homicide rates is a potentially different story. Although many of these homicides may indeed be mislabeled intimate partner or family killings, homicides of acquaintances also include those that involve out-of-control fights, gang-related killings, and other situations that more closely resemble the image of men's homicide. These homicides are related less to the amount of women's inequality in the domestic sphere and more to the social

and ecological features of public space. Therefore, the possible utility of gender-central explanations in understanding women's acquaintance homicide is less clear.

More specifically, the questions are, How much can indicators of
gender equality improve upon traditional predictors in explaining
women's homicide, and What is the best possible explanation for
women's homicide rates given the study data? These questions were
addressed using the overall women's homicide offending rates and
those of acquaintance, family, and stranger victims, as discussed previously. The first question considers improving on traditional explanations built on the analyses presented in Chapter 3. Significant indicators from the traditional equations were retained. These indicators,
in addition to the control variables of the percentage of women ages
15–39 and population size, were reexamined with regression analyses of women's city-level homicide rates by victim-offender relationship.[1]

Once a baseline of the most useful model of the traditional variables was established, the two sets of gender equality variables were
added to the equation. First, indicators of economic equality/inequal-
ity were added, including the rate of women's employment, gender
equality in employment, gender equality in income, and the percentage of working women in managerial and technical professions. An
indicator of a lack of economic opportunity and low economic gender equality was included as the percentage of female single-headed
households with children that are poor. As discussed previously,
these are the best measures available from the census to represent
women's levels of opportunity and, conversely, disadvantage, economic equality relative to men, and occupational prestige.

The final set of variables added to the equation was that of social
equality—equality in social roles, expectations, and structures. As
discussed earlier, social equality can be measured only through the
indirect evidence that it may exist. Finding data to create the measures is difficult, and perhaps more than any others these variables
should be viewed with caution appropriate to the use of secondary
data and imprecise measurement of concepts. The variables used to
indicate social equality included the percentage of single-parent
households with children headed by men, the rate of cohabitation,
and the percentage of women who were divorced or separated.

These social indicators are argued to indicate the amount of
shared responsibility in child rearing and the degree of emphasis on

the traditional institution of marriage. Men's parenting could be measured only with the single-headed household measure. Thus it is argued that the greater the percentage of single-parent households with children that are headed by men, the more the responsibility of child rearing is shared by men and women. This would contrast with traditional demands that women raise children, particularly after divorce.

The measures used for traditional marriage expectations were again derived from available data reflecting current marital and relationship status for a city's population. It is argued that greater rates of cohabitation reflect the acceptability of couples living in nontraditional partner relationships and the comfort with which cohabiting couples would report their relationships to the census. Greater percentages of women divorced and separated, we can argue, represent the percentage of women who live outside the traditional expectation that women will get (and stay) married to men. In summary, these two indicators theoretically indicate how much persons living in a city experience a social climate in which there is release from traditional constraints of formal marriage.

The final regression model included traditional predictors and controls, economic inequality indicators, and social equality indicators. As each additional group of variables was added, an F score for change in $R^2$ was computed to see if these additions as a whole were statistically significant.[2] This is necessary to explore if in fact gender equality variables can add to the existing ability to explain women's homicide offending. Thus to determine the success of these collections of variables, one would look for significant increases in $R^2$, which would indicate important increases in the amount of women's homicide offending that is explained.

After the question of overall improvement is addressed, the question of the best model building remains. The final results from the previous analysis were subjected to stepwise regression to show which variables are most useful in an explanatory model of women's homicide offending overall and for intimate partners, family members, and acquaintances. The variables indicated as significant in this procedure were then, in the interest of parsimony, rerun with the control variables of population size and the percentage of those ages 15–39. The final model, then is the best possible explanation for each women's homicide offending type given the traditional and gender equality variables included in the analysis.[3]

## Gender Equality and Women's Overall Homicide Rates

Gender equality and the overall homicide rate were the first to be explored. Traditional predictors were reanalyzed for the baseline model (see Table B.1 in Appendix B).

Of the eight traditional variables, three were significant enough to retain for the gender equality analysis, as shown in Table 4.1. In Equation 1 heterogeneity (percentage African American), poverty, and percentage of the population divorced or separated increased the overall women's homicide rate. The control variables were insignificant. This collection of traditional variables explained a modest 45.7 percent of the overall women's homicide offending rate.

Economic equality was a significant addition to the traditional model for predicting women's overall homicide rates. Although the majority of the indicators were insignificant, gender equality in income significantly decreased women's homicide rates. More important, this collection of indicators significantly increased $R^2$, from 0.457 to 0.478. In other words, there was a 2.1 percent increase in explaining women's overall homicide offending rates with the

**Table 4.1　Gender Equality Models and Women's Total Homicide Rates, Equation 1 (retained traditional variables)**

| Variable | b | Beta | p |
|---|---|---|---|
| Log of percentage African American | 0.222 | 0.343 | <0.001 |
| Percentage of families in poverty | 0.037 | 0.263 | <0.001 |
| Percentage of total population divorced or separated | 0.083 | 0.206 | 0.003 |
| Percentage female 15–39 | –0.014 | –0.054 | 0.360 |
| Population size (1990) | <0.001 | 0.040 | 0.482 |
| Female employment rate | — | — | — |
| Gender equality in employment | — | — | — |
| Gender equality in income | — | — | — |
| Percentage of working women in managerial and technical professions | — | — | — |
| Percentage of female single-headed households with children that are poor | — | — | — |
| Percentage of male single-headed households with children | — | — | — |
| Rate of cohabiting couples per 100,000 | — | — | — |
| Percentage of women divorced or separated | — | — | — |
| Adjusted $R^2$ | | 0.457 | |
| Significance of F ($R^2$) | | <0.001 | |
| F score for model | | | |
| Improvement | | — | |
| Significance of F | | — | |

**Table 4.1** **(continued) Gender Equality Models and Women's Total Homicide Rates, Equation 2 (economic equality variables added)**

| Variable | b | Beta | p |
|---|---|---|---|
| Log of percentage African American | 0.150 | 0.231 | 0.010 |
| Percentage of families in poverty | 0.010 | 0.068 | 0.615 |
| Percentage of total population divorced or separated | 0.114 | 0.282 | <0.001 |
| Percentage female 15–39 | −0.007 | 0.028 | 0.703 |
| Population size (1990) | <0.001 | 0.071 | 0.228 |
| Female employment rate | <−0.001 | −0.159 | 0.112 |
| Gender equality in employment | 0.015 | 0.114 | 0.114 |
| Gender equality in income | −0.021 | −0.170 | 0.015 |
| Percentage of working women in managerial and technical professions | 0.010 | 0.067 | 0.342 |
| Percentage of female single-headed households with children that are poor | 0.075 | 0.236 | 0.073 |
| Percentage of male single-headed households with children | — | — | — |
| Rate of cohabiting couples per 100,000 | — | — | — |
| Percentage of women divorced or separated | — | — | — |
| Adjusted $R^2$ | | 0.478 | |
| Significance of F ($R^2$) | | <0.001 | |
| F score for model | | | |
| Improvement | | 2.39 | |
| Significance of F | | 0.05 | |

**Table 4.1** **(continued) Gender Equality Models and Women's Total Homicide Rates, Equation 3 (social equality variables added)**

| Variable | b | Beta | p |
|---|---|---|---|
| Log of percentage African American | 0.115 | 0.177 | 0.075 |
| Percentage of families in poverty | <0.001 | 0.006 | 0.970 |
| Percentage of total population divorced or separated | 0.483 | 1.199 | <0.001 |
| Percentage female 15–39 | 0.032 | 0.125 | 0.099 |
| Population size (1990) | <0.001 | 0.071 | 0.213 |
| Female employment rate | <−0.001 | −0.211 | 0.058 |
| Gender equality in employment | 0.010 | 0.074 | 0.344 |
| Gender equality in income | −0.007 | −0.055 | 0.500 |
| Percentage of working women in managerial and technical professions | 0.016 | 0.104 | 0.141 |
| Percentage of female single-headed households with children that are poor | 0.068 | 0.213 | 0.096 |
| Percentage of male single-headed households with children | −.001 | −0.009 | 0.937 |
| Rate of cohabiting couples per 100,000 | <−0.001 | −0.224 | 0.003 |
| Percentage of women divorced or separated | −0.308 | −0.789 | 0.005 |
| Adjusted $R^2$ | | 0.511 | |
| Significance of F ($R^2$) | | <0.001 | |
| F score for model | | | |
| Improvement | | 4.73 | |
| Significance of F | | 0.01 | |

*Note:* Overall improvement from traditional predictors to full model: F = 3.36 (p = <0.001).

inclusion of the economic variables. Although this increase may seem small, it is statistically significant.

Social equality variables improved upon the prediction power of the model including both traditional and economic variables. Overall, social equality significantly decreased the women's homicide rate. The cohabitation rate and percentage of women divorced or separated significantly decreased women's homicide offending. Because of multicollinearity, however, the negative relationship observed in the percentage of women divorced or separated is suspect. The percentage of the total population divorced or separated minus the percentage of women divorced or separated is significant and positive. In the absence of the percentage of those divorced or separated, the percentage of women divorced or separated becomes positive and significant. Thus a relationship exists between family instability and women's total homicide offending rates, but it is unclear what unique contribution women's divorce and separation has. The power of the social equality indicators was evident in a significant increase in $R^2$ from 0.478 to 0.511. This model was a 3.3 percent improvement over the model with economic equality and traditional variables alone.

A look at gender equality and women's overall homicide rates finds that both economic and social equality levels play a major role in the rate at which women in cities kill. The addition of all equality variables improved the amount of variance explained by 5.4 percent. This additional prediction power was very significant at less than 0.001. Thus any explanation of the rate of women's overall homicide must include indicators reflecting women's economic and social status.

Combining types of homicide into aggregated rates, however, masks important differences between them. It is difficult to argue that the circumstances behind the killing of family members would be the same as those behind acquaintance killing. Thus although equality is important in women's overall rate of killing, it is necessary to examine how it may differ among intimate partner, family member, and acquaintance killing rates.

## Gender Equality and Women's
## Intimate Partner Homicide Rates

First, the traditional analysis was redone (see Table B.2 in Appendix B for these results), and the best traditional predictors were kept for the analysis of women's intimate partner homicide rates. (See Table 4.2.)

Individually, the traditional predictors were better predictors for women's intimate partner homicide offending rates than for women's rates overall. From the traditional predictors population density, the percentage of African Americans, poverty, and the percentage of those divorced or separated were retained for the baseline analysis. In this initial equation divorced and separated became insignificant, indicating that the other nonincluded traditional variables had enhanced its effect. Population density, contrary to traditional prediction and as we saw previously, significantly decreases women's intimate homicide rate. Overall, the retained predictors explained 31.9 percent of women's rates of killing intimate partners.

Economic equality adds little to our ability to explain women's rate of intimate partner killing. That ability increases by only 1 percent, which for this equation is statistically insignificant. The female employment rate individually decreases women's intimate partner

Table 4.2  **Gender Equality Models and Women's Intimate Partner Homicide Rates, Equation 1 (retained traditional variables)**

| Variable | b | Beta | p |
|---|---|---|---|
| Log of population density | –0.195 | –0.208 | 0.003 |
| Log of percentage African American | 0.127 | 0.250 | 0.002 |
| Percentage of families in poverty | 0.028 | 0.254 | 0.002 |
| Percentage of total population divorced or separated | 0.040 | 0.129 | 0.094 |
| Percentage female 15–39 | –0.025 | –0.124 | 0.063 |
| Population size (1990) | <0.001 | 0.041 | 0.535 |
| Female employment rate | — | — | — |
| Gender equality in employment | — | — | — |
| Gender equality in income | — | — | — |
| Percentage of working women in managerial and technical professions | — | — | — |
| Percentage of female single-headed households with children that are poor | — | — | — |
| Percentage of male single-headed households with children | — | — | — |
| Rate of cohabiting couples per 100,000 | — | — | — |
| Percentage of women divorced or separated | — | — | — |
| Adjusted $R^2$ | | 0.319 | |
| Significance of F ($R^2$) | | <0.001 | |
| F score for model | | | |
| Improvement | | — | |
| Significance of F | | — | |

**Table 4.2    (continued) Gender Equality Models and Women's Intimate Partner Homicide Rates, Equation 2 (economic equality variables added)**

| Variable | b | Beta | p |
|---|---|---|---|
| Log of population density | −0.179 | −0.191 | 0.019 |
| Log of percentage African American | 0.094 | 0.186 | 0.067 |
| Percentage of families in poverty | <−0.001 | −0.008 | 0.957 |
| Percentage of total population divorced or separated | 0.059 | 0.187 | 0.036 |
| Percentage female 15–39 | −0.025 | −0.128 | 0.124 |
| Population size (1990) | <0.001 | 0.026 | 0.696 |
| Female employment rate | <−0.001 | −0.279 | 0.015 |
| Gender equality in employment | 0.011 | 0.110 | 0.179 |
| Gender equality in income | <0.001 | 0.002 | 0.979 |
| Percentage of working women in managerial and technical professions | 0.010 | 0.086 | 0.283 |
| Percentage of female single-headed households with children that are poor | 0.030 | 0.122 | 0.418 |
| Percentage of male single-headed households with children | — | — | — |
| Rate of cohabiting couples per 100,000 | — | — | — |
| Percentage of women divorced or separated | — | — | — |
| Adjusted $R^2$ | | 0.329 | |
| Significance of F ($R^2$) | | <0.001 | |
| F score for model | | | |
|   Improvement | | 1.53 | |
|   Significance of F | | NS | |

**Table 4.2    (continued) Gender Equality Models and Women's Intimate Partner Homicide Rates, Equation 3 (social equality variables added)**

| Variable | b | Beta | p |
|---|---|---|---|
| Log of population density | −0.131 | −0.140 | 0.123 |
| Log of percentage African American | 0.092 | 0.182 | 0.111 |
| Percentage of families in poverty | −0.002 | −0.017 | 0.925 |
| Percentage of total population divorced or separated | 0.395 | 1.257 | <0.001 |
| Percentage female 15–39 | −0.008 | −0.040 | 0.660 |
| Population size (1990) | <0.001 | 0.019 | 0.778 |
| Female employment rate | <−0.001 | −0.318 | 0.013 |
| Gender equality in employment | 0.009 | 0.089 | 0.329 |
| Gender equality in income | 0.005 | 0.047 | 0.651 |
| Percentage of working women in managerial and technical professions | 0.017 | 0.140 | 0.083 |
| Percentage of female single-headed households with children that are poor | 0.031 | 0.126 | 0.399 |
| Percentage of male single-headed households with children | 0.011 | 0.095 | 0.463 |
| Rate of cohabiting couples per 100,000 | <−0.001 | −0.175 | 0.067 |
| Percentage of women divorced or separated | −0.294 | −0.968 | 0.003 |
| Adjusted $R^2$ | | 0.360 | |
| Significance of F ($R^2$) | | <0.001 | |
| F score for model | | | |
|   Improvement | | 3.33 | |
|   Significance of F | | 0.05 | |

*Note:* Overall improvement from traditional predictors to full model: $F = 2.15$ ($p = 0.05$).

homicide offending significantly, which suggests that economic opportunity, not relative status as shown in employment and income equality, is more important in decreasing women's intimate partner killing rates. In the context of what we know about domestic violence, this makes sense. One of battered women's most important needs is access to financial resources and the empowerment that comes from working. This need can be seen in the power of the women's employment rate to decrease women's intimate partner homicide offending. If women have greater access to economic opportunity, they are more likely to be able to get out of a battering situation before it becomes lethal. Measures such as equality in employment and income reflect a relative disadvantage that in itself might not keep a woman in a battering situation if women's absolute status is high enough to provide the resources to allow her to make it on her own.

Social equality, however, does significantly improve upon traditional and economic equality predictors. $R^2$ increases significantly from 0.329 to 0.360 with the addition of social equality indicators. In other words, there is a 3.1 percent improvement in the ability to explain women's killing of intimate partners by adding social equality to traditional variables and economic equality. The percentage of women divorced or separated significantly decreases women's rate of killing intimate partners. When the percentage of the population divorced or separated is examined alone, it is significantly and positively related to women's intimate partner killing rates. The percentage of women divorced or separated is insignificant when included alone. Thus the relationship between the percentage of women divorced or separated and women's intimate partner homicide rates can be attributable to multicollinearity and not to any independent effect of women's divorce or separation. The cohabitation rate approaches a similar significant, negative relationship.

Women's intimate partner homicide rates exhibit a different pattern than was observed in the aggregated rates. Equality indicators significantly increased the ability to explain rates of intimate partner killing from the traditional to the full model of those rates, but this is completely a result of social equality variables. Thus for cities, it appears that the breakdown of traditional marriage norms and expectations does more to decrease women's intimate partner homicide offending rates than economic equalities between men and women as a whole.

## Gender Equality and Women's Family Homicide Rates

For the gender equality analysis of women's family homicide rates, the traditional predictors were rerun (see Table B.3 in Appendix B), and the best indicator was selected. Traditional predictors were extremely poor in predicting family homicide offending rates for women. Only one predictor—the percentage divorced and separated—was retained. The variables retained explained only 17.3 percent of women's rates of killing family members. (See Table 4.3.)

Economic equality variables added considerable explanatory power beyond traditional predictors. $R^2$ increased from 0.173 to 0.257, a highly significant increase of 8.4 percent in the ability to explain women's family homicide rates. Although beginning with a low amount of explanation using traditional variables would help to explain this large improvement, the impoverishment of the traditional model indicates that variables such as equality variables are needed to better understand this kind of homicide. Gender equality in income significantly decreased women's rates of family killing, whereas the percentage of female single-headed households that

**Table 4.3    Gender Equality Models and Women's Family Homicide Rates, Equation 1 (retained traditional variables)**

| Variable | b | Beta | p |
|---|---|---|---|
| Percentage of total population divorced or separated | 0.088 | 0.388 | <0.001 |
| Percentage female 15–39 | –0.011 | –0.079 | 0.260 |
| Population size (1990) | <0.001 | 0.095 | 0.165 |
| Female employment rate | — | — | — |
| Gender equality in employment | — | — | — |
| Gender equality in income | — | — | — |
| Percentage of working women in managerial and technical professions | — | — | — |
| Percentage of female single-headed households with children that are poor | — | — | — |
| Percentage of male single-headed households with children | — | — | — |
| Rate of cohabiting couples per 100,000 | — | — | — |
| Percentage of women divorced or separated | — | — | — |
| Adjusted $R^2$ | | 0.173 | |
| Significance of F ($R^2$) | | <0.001 | |
| F score for model | | | |
| Improvement | | — | |
| Significance of F | | — | |

**Table 4.3** (continued) Gender Equality Models and Women's Family Homicide Rates, Equation 2 (economic equality variables added)

| Variable | b | Beta | p |
|---|---|---|---|
| Percentage of total population divorced or separated | 0.073 | 0.327 | <0.001 |
| Percentage female 15–39 | 0.005 | 0.032 | 0.698 |
| Population size (1990) | <0.001 | 0.070 | 0.318 |
| Female employment rate | <–0.001 | –0.040 | 0.688 |
| Gender equality in employment | <0.001 | 0.013 | 0.880 |
| Gender equality in income | –0.013 | –0.180 | 0.029 |
| Percentage of working women in managerial and technical professions | 0.009 | 0.103 | 0.219 |
| Percentage of female single-headed households with children that are poor | 0.067 | 0.377 | <0.001 |
| Percentage of male single-headed households with children | — | — | — |
| Rate of cohabiting couples per 100,000 | — | — | — |
| Percentage of women divorced or separated | — | — | — |
| Adjusted $R^2$ | | 0.257 | |
| Significance of F ($R^2$) | | <0.001 | |
| F score for model | | | |
| Improvement | | 4.95 | |
| Significance of F | | <0.001 | |

**Table 4.3** (continued) Gender Equality Models and Women's Family Homicide Rates, Equation 3 (social equality variables added)

| Variable | b | Beta | p |
|---|---|---|---|
| Percentage of total population divorced or separated | 0.252 | 1.116 | 0.002 |
| Percentage female 15–39 | 0.015 | 0.104 | 0.222 |
| Population size (1990) | <0.001 | 0.069 | 0.319 |
| Female employment rate | <–0.001 | –0.052 | 0.608 |
| Gender equality in employment | <0.001 | 0.006 | 0.948 |
| Gender equality in income | –0.008 | –0.113 | 0.228 |
| Percentage of working women in managerial and technical professions | 0.012 | 0.143 | 0.094 |
| Percentage of female single-headed households with children that are poor | 0.069 | 0.383 | 0.004 |
| Percentage of male single-headed households with children | 0.009 | –0.101 | 0.348 |
| Rate of cohabiting couples per 100,000 | <–0.001 | –0.198 | 0.026 |
| Percentage of women divorced or separated | –0.152 | –0.694 | 0.041 |
| Adjusted $R^2$ | | 0.277 | |
| Significance of F ($R^2$) | | <0.001 | |
| F score for model | | | |
| Improvement | | 2.52 | |
| Significance of F | | NS | |

*Note:* Overall improvement from traditional predictors to full model: $F = 4.12$ ($p = <0.001$).

were poor significantly increased it. The most important finding is the increased level of overall explanation using economic equality variables.

Social equality, however, did not improve significantly on this model. The amount of variance explained increased by only 2 percent, which is insignificant in this model. The cohabitation rate and women's percentage of divorced and separated did, however, significantly decrease women's family homicide offending rates individually. With regard to the percentage of women divorced or separated, we see the same confounding as we saw in the women's total homicide rate analysis. Alone, the percentage of women divorced or separated is significant and positive. Thus a relationship between women's divorce and separation and the rate of family killing is present, but it is unclear how that relationship works. Interestingly, increased parity in single heading of households by gender did not impact women's rates of killing family members.

Overall, equality predictors significantly improve the ability to explain women's family homicide rates, although this increase is largely the result of the economic equality variables. This suggests that financial resources to assist the women may be more important in decreasing women's family homicide offending rates than is the loosening of traditional gender expectations. Given the limitations in the measurement of the gender equality variables, these findings (as with all presented here) are only suggestive of relationships that need further and more precise exploration.

## Gender Equality and Women's Acquaintance Homicide Rates

Finally, the relationship between gender equality and women's acquaintance homicide rates was analyzed. First, the traditional predictors were reanalyzed (see Table B.4 in Appendix B).

Several of the traditional predictors were kept for the analysis of acquaintance homicide, as presented in Table 4.4. Poverty, the South, and the percentage of divorced or separated all significantly increased women's acquaintance homicide rates. A higher percentage of change, contrary to traditional prediction, decreased women's acquaintance homicide rates. Of the two control variables, the percentage of women ages 15–39 significantly increased women's

**Table 4.4   Gender Equality Models and Women's Acquaintance Homicide Rates, Equation 1 (retained traditional variables)**

| Variable | b | Beta | p |
|---|---|---|---|
| Percentage of families in poverty | 0.023 | 0.222 | 0.005 |
| Log of percentage change | −0.732 | −0.206 | 0.005 |
| Confederate South | 0.329 | 0.250 | <0.001 |
| Percentage of total population divorced or separated | 0.071 | 0.241 | <0.001 |
| Percentage female 15–39 | 0.026 | 0.140 | 0.037 |
| Population size (1990) | <0.001 | 0.109 | 0.082 |
| Female employment rate | — | — | — |
| Gender equality in employment | — | — | — |
| Gender equality in income | — | — | — |
| Percentage of working women in managerial and technical professions | — | — | — |
| Percentage of female single-headed households with children that are poor | — | — | — |
| Percentage of male single-headed households with children | — | — | — |
| Rate of cohabiting couples per 100,000 | — | — | — |
| Percentage of women divorced or separated | — | — | — |
| Adjusted $R^2$ | | 0.339 | |
| Significance of F ($R^2$) | | <0.001 | |
| F score for model | | | |
| Improvement | | — | |
| Significance of F | | — | |

**Table 4.4   (continued) Gender Equality Models and Women's Acquaintance Homicide Rates, Equation 2 (economic equality variables added)**

| Variable | b | Beta | p |
|---|---|---|---|
| Percentage of families in poverty | 0.019 | 0.184 | 0.281 |
| Log of percentage change | −0.724 | −0.204 | 0.023 |
| Confederate South | 0.321 | 0.230 | <0.001 |
| Percentage of total population divorced or separated | 0.078 | 0.262 | 0.001 |
| Percentage female 15–39 | 0.038 | 0.207 | 0.018 |
| Population size (1990) | <0.001 | 0.141 | 0.037 |
| Female employment rate | <−0.001 | −0.018 | 0.881 |
| Gender equality in employment | 0.004 | 0.039 | 0.643 |
| Gender equality in income | −0.011 | −0.120 | 0.138 |
| Percentage of working women in managerial and technical professions | −0.006 | −0.052 | 0.525 |
| Percentage of female single-headed households with children that are poor | 0.012 | 0.049 | 0.710 |
| Percentage of male single-headed households with children | — | — | — |
| Rate of cohabiting couples per 100,000 | — | — | — |
| Percentage of women divorced or separated | — | — | — |
| Adjusted $R^2$ | | 0.330 | |
| Significance of F ($R^2$) | | <0.001 | |
| F score for model | | | |
| Improvement | | 0.55 | |
| Significance of F | | NS | |

**Table 4.4**    **(continued) Gender Equality Models and Women's Acquaintance Homicide Rates, Equation 3 (social equality variables added)**

| Variable | b | Beta | p |
|---|---|---|---|
| Percentage of families in poverty | 0.008 | 0.074 | 0.688 |
| Log of percentage change | −0.688 | −0.193 | 0.044 |
| Confederate South | 0.367 | 0.262 | 0.003 |
| Percentage of total population divorced or separated | −0.013 | −0.043 | 0.907 |
| Percentage female 15–39 | 0.032 | 0.171 | 0.072 |
| Population size (1990) | <0.001 | 0.141 | 0.037 |
| Female employment rate | <−0.001 | −0.077 | 0.558 |
| Gender equality in employment | <−0.001 | −0.008 | 0.931 |
| Gender equality in income | −0.008 | −0.085 | 0.370 |
| Percentage of working women in managerial and technical professions | −0.010 | −0.087 | 0.298 |
| Percentage of female single-headed households with children that are poor | −0.006 | −0.024 | 0.862 |
| Percentage of male single-headed households with children | −0.022 | −0.190 | 0.115 |
| Rate of cohabiting couples per 100,000 | <0.001 | 0.089 | 0.413 |
| Percentage of women divorced or separated | 0.079 | 0.276 | 0.420 |
| Adjusted $R^2$ | | 0.331 | |
| Significance of F ($R^2$) | | <0.001 | |
| F score for model | | | |
| Improvement | | 1.15 | |
| Significance of F | | NS | |

*Note:* Overall improvement from traditional predictors to full model: F = 0.80 (p = NS).

acquaintance homicide rates. Traditional-control variables explained 33.9 percent of the rate at which women kill acquaintances.

Neither economic nor social equality increased the ability to explain women's acquaintance homicide offending rates beyond the explanatory power of traditional predictors. In fact, explanatory power, as measured by the adjusted $R^2$, decreased with the addition of equality predictors. Furthermore, none of the equality predictors even approached significance, whereas most of the traditional predictors retained their significant effects. The percentage of families in poverty and percentage of the population separated or divorced ceased to be significant only when their gender equality counterparts were added. The high association between overall poverty and the overall percentage of those divorced or separated and poor single mothers and the percentage of women divorced or separated statistically eliminated significant relationships of either group. This was confirmed when analyses were run including only one of each pair. For each, the gender-sensitive indicator became significant and positive in the absence of the other, and vice versa.

Therefore, gender equality is not useful for increasing our understanding of women's acquaintance homicide offending rates. Statistically, these gender variables decrease rather than increase variance explained. Theoretically, this is not surprising. Acquaintance homicide, by definition, does not involve persons with whom the offender has a close relationship. These relationships are less likely to be subject to oppressive domestic conditions in which women may be trapped by abuse and a lack of resources for caregiving assistance or be compelled to live out restrictive, traditional gender roles around the home and intimacy. Thus these conditions are less likely to influence friendships and more distant familiar relationships, which are more freely entered and exited and do not require intense caretaking.

Understanding women's homicide rates as a whole benefits from a consideration of gender equality in both economic and social terms. For overall homicide rates, significant improvements in explained variance were observed with the addition of both economic equality and social equality predictors. The aggregated, compiled nature of overall homicide rate calculation, however, did mask important differences by homicide context. Explaining the rate of intimate partner killing was improved significantly only by social equality predictors, thus indicating that as a rule, women's intimate partner homicide offending rates are lower not when economic equalities and opportunities are more available but when traditional social demands for legal marriage are followed less. The importance of the female employment rate in decreasing intimate partner homicides is notable despite the overall performance of economic equality variables.

Explaining the women's rate of family killing, in contrast, was significantly improved only by economic equality, thus suggesting that the lack of access to and equity in economic resources was a much greater factor in general than traditional gender expectations. The lack of gender equality effects in acquaintance homicide offending rates was not unanticipated. Acquaintance homicides by women would seem to fit more squarely with the image of homicide assumed in traditional theories. These differences among types of women's homicides remind us that the context of offending is as important as the gender of the offender.

In general, social and economic equality have negative associations with women's homicide offending rates, thus indicating that women's equality can serve as a powerful force in decreasing their rates of lethal violence. Economic equality variables had few individual effects, although the female employment rate significantly decreased the rate of women's intimate partner homicides. The percentage of female single-headed households that are poor (a reverse variable for gender equality) significantly increased the rate of women's family killing. The rest of the economic equality variables individually had little effect. The lack of effect of individual variables, however, was likely an indication of high correlations with other variables (multicollinearity).

Social equality variables had much more consistently significant negative associations with women's homicide offending rates. The cohabitation rate significantly decreased women's overall and family homicide offending rates and approached significance for women's intimate partner rates. The percentage of male single-headed households significantly decreased women's total homicide offending rates. The percentage of women divorced or separated was significantly and negatively associated with women's total, intimate partner, and family homicide rates, but it is difficult to determine whether this is an actual relationship or one resulting from the high association between this indicator and the percentage of the total population divorced or separated.

Gender equality, in terms of both economics and social expectations, is indeed valuable for improving explanations of women's homicide offending in the domestic sphere. The fact that traditional models have ignored these considerations stands as an empirical and theoretical weakness in their considerations of homicide. The next logical step, then, is to build the best possible explanation for women's rates of homicide offending using the variables included in the analysis conducted here.

## Modeling Women's Homicide Rates

Because of the differences observed in the various victim-offender relationships, the best possible model of women's homicide offending will vary depending on what kind of homicide is being explained.

The process for model building includes a consideration of both traditional and gender equality indicators and draws upon the previously reported analysis. Stepwise regression analysis was conducted with the indicators from the complete model of retained traditional, economic equality, and social equality indicators to produce the best possible model for explaining women's overall, intimate partner, family, and acquaintance killing rates. Control variables of population size and the percentage of women ages 15–39 were added to these variables.

Although the use of stepwise regression for model building is often criticized for being atheoretical, the use of it here is not. It has been demonstrated that several traditional and gender equality variables may have significant effects on women's rates of homicide. The importance of gender equality has been demonstrated theoretically and empirically. Many of these variables, however, have confounding relationships with each other that statistically cloud the explanation of women's homicide offending rates. We can look at a collection of variables for overall improvement, as we did previously, but it is important to examine individual effects as well. To do this, it is necessary to pull the most statistically significant predictors out of the overall mix. Stepwise regression allows us to do this.

## Modeling Women's Overall Homicide Rates

The overall women's homicide offending rate was modeled first. The stepwise regression analysis created a model of both traditional and gender equality indicators. (See Table 4.5.)

The variables of the percentage of African Americans and the percentage of families in poverty significantly increased women's overall homicide offending rates. Thus as heterogeneity in a city increases, women commit homicide at a greater rate. As the percentage of families in poverty increases, the greater the women's homicide offending rate. What is important about overall poverty is that it emerges as more significant than the percentage of women in poverty. This suggests that the structural condition of poverty as a whole affects the lives of women more than the direct effects of the likelihood of single women living in poverty. That is, poverty creates a context that has a more general and encompassing effect on its inhabitants, both men and women.

**Table 4.5    Model for Women's Total Homicide Rates**

| Variable | b | Beta | p |
|---|---|---|---|
| Percentage divorced or separated | 0.441 | 1.094 | <0.001 |
| Log of percentage African American | 0.180 | 0.271 | <0.001 |
| Percentage of families in poverty | 0.036 | 0.251 | <0.001 |
| Percentage females divorced or separated | –0.290 | –0.743 | 0.003 |
| Rate of cohabiting couples per 100,000 | <–0.001 | –0.242 | <0.001 |
| Population size (1990) | <0.001 | 0.073 | 0.180 |
| Percentage female 15–39 | 0.024 | 0.096 | 0.154 |
| Adjusted $R^2$ | | 0.502 | |
| Significance of F ($R^2$) | | <0.001 | |

Family instability, measured by the percentage of the population divorced or separated, significantly increases women's homicide offending rates overall, as shown in the model. The percentage of women divorced or separated, an indication of social equality, significantly decreases women's overall homicide offending rates. Because of high multicollinearity between these two variables, two additional analyses were run to sort out their real, relative effects. The first eliminated the overall divorced and separated indicator and left the indicator of the percentage of women divorced or separated. Without the overall measure, the female-specific measure became positive. The second analysis involved replacing the percentage of men divorced or separated for the overall indicator. In this analysis the percentage of men divorced or separated was significant and positive, but that of women divorced or separated failed to reach significance. Thus the distinct relationship between women's freedom through divorce and women's homicide offending is unclear. What can be said is that the percentage of all persons divorced or separated increases women's overall homicide offending. The percentage of women divorced or separated, although highly correlated to the overall measure, does retain some independent qualities that may represent women's freedom from traditional marriage. These issues cannot be addressed with the data here and indicate the challenge of getting precise and valid measures of gender equality.

In this model of women's overall homicide rates, the rate of cohabiting couples significantly decreases women's overall homicide offending rates. In other words, the more often couples reported living in nonmarital but committed relationships, the lower the rate of women's killing. One interpretation may be that cohabitation reflects an approach to everyday life that contrasts with traditionally held expectations for marriage. Cohabiting couples do not have marriage certificates and thus do not demonstrate the constraints of traditional marriage values. Additionally, living together out of wedlock allows more legal freedom to end the relationship. Places characterized by cohabitation have a climate of greater freedom that provides more options for women and fewer constraints to stay in bad situations. This interpretation applies directly to the intimate partner homicides embedded in the overall rate. The climate of freedom may also represent more generally a climate of women's social freedoms that may have positive influences on women's relationships with both family and acquaintances.

In the analytically created model, the control variables were insignificant, suggesting an influence of neither city size nor age structure on women's offending overall. This model of the strongest variables explained a modest 50.2 percent of our understanding of women's overall rates of killing, an improvement over the traditional homicide explanations that do not include gender. Much remains to be explained with more precise measures of gender equality and additional theoretical understandings of women and homicide.

## Modeling Women's Intimate Partner Homicide Rates

As discussed previously, the context of the victim-offender relationship must be taken into account in any discussion of homicide offending. Different relationships are affected by a somewhat different set of variables, as we have seen with previous analyses.

In building the best possible model for women's intimate homicide offending rates, some similarities and differences are found from the model for women's overall homicide offending rates. Like that model, the model for intimate homicide offending rates shows both traditional and gender equality variables. (See Table 4.6.)

As found in the modeling of overall women's homicide offending, the percentage of African Americans, as in overall homicide, significantly increases women's intimate partner offending rates. Thus heterogeneity leads to a climate in which women more frequently kill intimate partners as well as victims overall.

The confounding of the percentage of those divorced or separated and the percentage of women divorced or separated in this model

**Table 4.6    Model for Women's Intimate Partner Homicide Rates**

| Variable | b | Beta | p |
|---|---|---|---|
| Percentage divorced or separated | 0.402 | 1.280 | <0.001 |
| Log of percentage African American | 0.105 | 0.207 | 0.007 |
| Female employment rate | <–0.001 | –0.228 | 0.001 |
| Percentage females divorced or separated | –0.281 | –0.925 | 0.002 |
| Rate of cohabiting couples per 100,000 | <–0.001 | –0.222 | 0.005 |
| Population size (1990) | <0.001 | 0.019 | 0.759 |
| Percentage female 15–39 | 0.006 | 0.032 | 0.679 |
| Adjusted $R^2$ | | 0.351 | |
| Significance of F ($R^2$) | | <0.001 | |

is similar to what we saw in the modeling of the overall rate. Additional analyses were conducted as in the overall analysis, and identical results were obtained. It is unclear if women's divorce and separation has a unique effect on women's intimate partner homicide offending rates, but the significance of the overall percentage of the population divorced or separated shows that familial disruption can play a role in rates of intimate partner killing by women. The fact that divorce and separation increase the risk of violence against women must be considered, as many killings of intimate partners by women occur in the context of self-defense. Therefore although the variable is derived from the traditional argument of community breakdown, the alternative explanation of this finding from a woman-centered perspective includes features of women's lives and violence against them.

This model building of women's intimate partner homicide rates shows evidence that both economic equality and social equality are important and statistically significant explanations of such killing. The cohabitation rate, similar to the analysis of women's offending rates overall, significantly decreases the rate at which women kill intimate partners. Thus the greater the number of persons who enter into nontraditional partnerships, the lower the rate of intimate partner killing by women. The releasing of traditional marriage expectations, as discussed previously, may provide fewer restrictions for women who need to get out of abusive situations. Additionally, it may represent more nontraditional views about men's and women's partnership roles and may decrease the likelihood of abusive situations.

In addition to the cohabitation rate, the female employment rate also emerges as a significant variable in understanding women's killing of intimate partners. As women's employment rates go up, the intimate partner homicide offending rate significantly decreases. Thus the more women participate in the economic sphere, the lower the rate of partner killing. Given that many intimate partner homicides are committed by women in the context of domestic abuse, this finding clearly points to the value of economic resources in providing opportunity and nonlethal options for women in stressful and abusive partnerships.

Gender equality plays an important role in understanding women's intimate partner homicide offending. Although the effects of heterogeneity suggest there may be some validity to this traditional explanation of women's killing of intimate partners, the largest contribution to explanation was seen in nontraditional beliefs and behaviors in partnerships and the importance of women's economic resources and participation in decreasing women's rate of intimate partner killing. As the best variables model explained only 35.1 percent of the rate of intimate partner killing by women, however, more remains to be explained. Again, more precise measures may contribute to improving the ability to explain why women kill. Additionally, given the intertwined relationship between women's and men's intimate homicide, some of the missing explanation is likely wrapped up in understanding domestic violence prior to its ultimate lethal outcomes.

To investigate the role of men's violence against women in understanding women's intimate partner homicide offending, the best variables model was rerun with men's intimate partner offending rates included as an independent variable. This variable is the closest possible proxy to men's violence against women. (See Table 4.7.)

In this analysis, adding men's violence to the model increases the explanatory power of the model by 4.6 percent, a highly statistically significant increase. Furthermore, it demonstrates that men's violence against women significantly increases women's rate of killing intimate partners. This finding supports the research that shows that women kill in this context largely in self-defense and as a result of abuse. The inclusion of men's violence against women in the model does not diminish any of the effects of social or economic gender equality. In other words, men's violence against women

**Table 4.7    Model for Women's Intimate Partner Homicide Rates, Including Men's Violence Against Women**

| Variable | b | Beta | p |
|---|---|---|---|
| Percentage divorced or separated | 0.366 | 1.166 | <0.001 |
| Log of percentage African American | <0.001 | 0.131 | 0.086 |
| Female employment rate | <−0.001 | −0.209 | 0.002 |
| Percentage females divorced or separated | −0.266 | −0.874 | 0.002 |
| Rate of cohabiting couples per 100,000 | <−0.001 | −0.191 | 0.013 |
| Log of men's intimate homicide rate | 0.216 | 0.257 | <0.001 |
| Population size (1990) | <−0.001 | −0.015 | 0.807 |
| Percentage female 15–39 | <0.001 | 0.035 | 0.637 |
| Adjusted $R^2$ | | 0.397 | |
| Significance of F ($R^2$) | | <0.001 | |

adds to the contributions of gender equality in understanding women's intimate homicide offending. The importance of the overall percentage of those divorced or separated does not change either, suggesting that it affects women's intimate partner killing not only through men's violence but independently. More research is needed to examine why this might be so. Interestingly, the role of heterogeneity in increasing women's rates of killing intimate partners disappears when men's violence is taken into account. Thus the percentage of African Americans affects men's use of violence against women but has no importance in women's killing of partners independent of that. Although the importance of men's violence against women in understanding women's intimate homicide offending is demonstrated, the more inclusive model still fails to explain more than 50 percent of women's intimate partner homicide offending.

## Modeling Women's Family Homicide Rates

Not surprisingly, the killing of family members by women involves a unique set of factors and is another situation that differs from women's killing of partners and killing overall. (See Table 4.8.)

When the best statistical model was created with stepwise regression, the only traditional variable that remained was the percentage of the population divorced or separated. This variable significantly increased women's family killing rate. Thus family disruption is a significant factor in that rate. It is interesting that women's per-

**Table 4.8   Model for Women's Family Homicide Rates**

| Variable | b | Beta | p |
|---|---|---|---|
| Percentage divorced or separated | 0.100 | 0.443 | <0.001 |
| Percentage of male single-headed households | −0.014 | −0.158 | 0.029 |
| Rate of cohabiting couples per 100,000 | <−0.001 | −0.215 | 0.009 |
| Population size (1990) | <0.001 | 0.097 | 0.143 |
| Percentage female 15–39 | 0.004 | 0.028 | 0.708 |
| Adjusted $R^2$ | | 0.231 | |
| Significance of F ($R^2$) | | <0.001 | |

centage of those divorced or separated does not appear. The possible differences between these variables were examined, as in the other analyses. When the overall divorced-separated measure was replaced with the women-specific measure, the women-specific rate was significant and positive. When the percentage of men divorced or separated was added, the women's percentage became nonsignificant but was still positive. It appears that overall amounts of divorce or separation create a climate in which women are more likely to kill family members. This could be associated with the stresses of single motherhood. Given the absence of any poverty effects (either the absolute or relative risk of single mothers), however, we cannot make a direct connection to the lack of resources. The stress, then, could come from more social elements involving divorce and separation, although this relationship merits closer study.

The social equality indicator of the percentage of male single-headed households with children helps explain the divorce finding. The greater the number of men heading single-headed households with children, the lower women's family homicide offending rates are. This measure could represent a breakdown of traditional gender expectations in child custody situations (as there is no male counterpart of the unwed mother). Traditionally, women have generally been expected to bear the responsibility for child rearing and the stigma associated with being a single mother. As men take on more single parenting, society makes a stronger statement about the need for men and women to take an equal part in child rearing. This creates circumstances in which women may be released from traditional constraints, which can create isolation, stress, and pressure. Because many women's family homicides are of children, lower stress can be seen to reduce the risk of this kind of killing. Also, as traditional child-rearing norms are closely related to other kinds of caregiving norms, reduced stress could have a more indirect effect on the risk to other family members and contribute to decreased family rates over-all.

The cohabitation rate also significantly decreased the women's family homicide offending rate, as it did for intimate partner and overall offending rates. This suggests that a higher rate of nontradi-tional couples has beneficial effects for women that decrease the risk of lethal violence against family members. One possible interpreta-tion of the cohabitation rate is that although it potentially represents nontraditional marriage-partnership forms, the rate may also reflect a more generally accepting environment with regard to women's domestic roles. The cohabitation rate could also serve as a proxy for a more generalized nontraditional orientation and greater support for women's social freedoms. The exact connection between the cohabi-tation rate and women's familial homicide offending calls for closer evaluation.

Overall, although economic variables added explanatory power in the first set of equations explaining women's family homicide offending rates, the most useful predictors were social equality indi-cators. Both of these indicators revealed that nontraditional living arrangements contribute to lower rates of women's killing of family members. Therefore the impact of gender equality in reducing the stress and difficulties in women's lives that may result in lethal vio-lence against family members cannot be denied. Given that the model with the best variables still explained only a little over 23 per-cent of the women's family homicide offending, however, much more work is needed to identify those factors that affect women who kill family members.

## Modeling Women's Acquaintance Homicide Rates

The previous analysis of acquaintance homicide offending rates showed that women's rates were best explained using traditional homicide predictors, unlike women's homicide offending in the domestic sphere of family and intimate partners. The stepwise regression model-building procedure revealed essentially the same picture. (See Table 4.9.)

Family disruption (percentage divorced or separated), the per-centage of families in poverty, and a city's location in the South all

**Table 4.9   Model for Women's Acquaintance Homicide Rates**

| Variable | b | Beta | p |
|---|---|---|---|
| Percentage divorced or separated | 0.069 | 0.233 | 0.001 |
| Percentage of families in poverty | 0.020 | 0.198 | 0.016 |
| Confederate South | 0.284 | 0.203 | 0.002 |
| Percentage of male single-headed households | −0.025 | −0.223 | 0.005 |
| Population size (1990) | <0.001 | 0.119 | 0.057 |
| Percentage female 15–39 | 0.021 | 0.114 | 0.079 |
| Adjusted $R^2$ | | 0.344 | |
| Significance of F ($R^2$) | | <0.001 | |

significantly increased women's acquaintance killing rates. These findings are highly consistent with traditional homicide predictions. Even the control variables—percentage of females ages 15–39 and population size—approach significance. Although on the macroanalytical level these factors seem to support the traditional, male-derived theories of homicide, the door may be open to gendered explanations that connect these variables to women's homicide offending against acquaintances. The strongest support, however, is seen for traditional homicide theory.

As the percentage of men heading households with children increased, women's acquaintance offending rate decreased. This indicates that despite the overwhelming influence of historically important factors in this type of women's homicide, the independent influence of equality in child custody also has an impact. The causal link, however, is much less clear. Many acquaintance homicides may be mislabeled killings of former lovers, and conflicts over the children and similar factors could precipitate them. In this scenario, more men taking responsibility for children more often could avert these conflicts. This issue requires further research, as the available data cannot address these questions.

Women's acquaintance homicide offending rates closely follow traditional homicide predictions. A strong interpretation of this finding is that an element of acquaintance homicide is likely more public and, as such, is more sensitive to overall community impacts. Additionally, the difference between women's acquaintance homicide offending and the other domestic forms further substantiates the importance of considering the victim-offender relationship in understanding women's homicide offending. The effect of the proportion of male single-headed households needs further study.

There is clearly a role for gender equality in modeling women's homicide offending rates, and its role clearly varies by victim-offender relationship. Compiling women's killing rates into an aggregate can obscure important differences. Depending on the victim-offender context, both economic and social measures of equality significantly decrease women's homicide offending rates. This is a clear indication that improving women's opportunity and equality results in better conditions for women's lives overall. Although gender equality significantly improves our ability to explain women's homicide offending rates, some crossover factors may affect both men and women. Further analysis, particularly qualitative, is needed to better understand the positive relationships between poverty, the percentage of African Americans, family disruption, and being in the South and women's offending rates. We need more information about how these factors affect cities to increase women's risk of lethal violence offending and how their lethal violence might resemble or differ from men's offending.

## Notes

1. The initial analysis of traditional predictors for these equations will be slightly different than the analysis described in Chapter 3. The percentage of females ages 15–39 was substituted for the overall population measure because of the focus on women in this analysis. The results with OLS regression of women's homicide offending rates regressed on the models with the percentage of females are reported in Tables B.1–B.4 of Appendix B. The significant variables in these equations were the baseline measure for the model building in this chapter.

2. The F-test for the change in $R^2$ was done with unadjusted $R^2$ because the formula contains a consideration of the number of independent variables in the equation. For considering purely the amount of variance explained, however, the adjusted $R^2$ is most appropriate, and that is what is reported.

3. Creating indicators for gender equality at the city level is difficult. The indicators used for these analyses reflect available data at the city level and, it is hoped, represent the best possible measurement of gender equality from obtainable sources. That does not mean these are the ideal measurements for gender equality, and they should not be taken as such.

# 5

# Extending Gender
# and Homicide Research

In both theory and analysis, considerations of gender opportunity and equality extend the ability to explain women's homicide offending. This study has shown that an examination of gender relations and structures helps explain how women differ from men in homicide offending. A study of gender also helps us to see how low equality and lack of opportunity for women can translate into situations that may encourage women's lethal violence.

The significance of gender for groups other than women, broadly defined, must also be pondered. The social impact of gender structures and relations can be felt by all persons, not just women. The research of Scott Coltrane (1994), James Messerschmidt (1993), R. W. Connell (1995), and Kenneth Polk (1994a, 1994b), for example, demonstrates that gender systems and relations affect men's lives as well. One might therefore surmise that the gender structures of women's opportunity and equality, inasmuch as they are representative of the larger gender system, could affect *men's* homicide offending. An examination of men who commit homicide should include not just men in general but diversity within men to encompass race and ethnicity, sexual orientation, class, and other ways in which men's lives can be differentially affected by gender.

A closer examination of the interaction among equality, opportunity, and women is a major step forward in understanding the conditions in which women generally are more likely to kill. However, to examine women as a singular group is to only examine a part of the picture. As Patricia Hill-Collins (1991), bell hooks (1984), Angela Davis (1981), and other feminists of color have argued, women of color often experience gender differently than white women. Additionally, important understandings of women who kill are also missed when we fail to consider the diversity sexual orientation, class, age, and other social dimensions provide. One general consideration of women masks important differences among women. Thus this chapter considers gender equality and homicide with respect to men and explores how gender equality may differ between groups of women.

## The Impact of Gender
## Equality on Men's Homicide Offending

Gender equality is a multifaceted concept that has value for understanding women's experiences with gender relations and structures and how they relate to women who kill. The value of considering men's experiences within a gender framework has only recently developed. The impact of gender equality on homicide by men has in particular not been largely addressed at the macro level. It is reasonable to argue that a pervasive social structure such as patriarchy would have an impact on men as well, including those who commit criminal acts. Some researchers have begun to examine masculinity and criminal men (e.g., Messerschmidt, 1993; Coggeshall, 1991; Newburn and Stanko, 1994; Bowker, 1998, Collier, 1998). Fewer have extended their study into homicide, although Polk (1994a, 1994b), for example, finds gender to be important in men's acts of homicide. Therefore, with respect to structural gender equality and the overall impact of gender on homicide, we need to ask, What about men?

### Theoretical Application of Gender
### Equality to Men's Homicide Offending

Gender equality has a strong potential for helping to explain men's homicide offending on societal and individual levels. Macrolevel gender inequality and equality are part of a societal system that cannot help but influence men's lives. The impact may be different in some ways than it is for women, but gender is also a central feature of men's status, experiences, and behavior. First, when gender equality is low, men's economic privilege is fostered. Thus gender equality between men and women in economic terms could threaten that privilege, resulting in an increase in male-perpetrated homicides as men respond to women's increased economic status and attempt to regain control where it seems to be lost.

Second, low gender equality fosters a system in which men have the right and expectation to control others around them in social relations. This control includes the enforcement of gender role segregation and the legitimation of men's violence against women and children. In this respect, gender equality could decrease men's domestic offending rates. Decreasing the legitimacy of men's violence against women means men will be less likely to be violent with their families and thus be less likely to kill when such killing would have been an escalation of abuse and violence. Also, gender equality could result in decreased stress created by traditional gender expectations of men. Whereas traditional notions of masculinity revolve around such hegemonic ideals as dominance, lack of "emotionality," and fulfilling provider roles (see, e.g., Connell, 1995), a more gender-equal society could relax these rigid social demands, allow for more flexibility in gender role playing for men, and ease some of the expectations that cause much stress for men (see, e.g., the role of class status and criminality in Messerschmidt, 1993).

## Empirical Exploration of Gender Equality and Men's Homicide Offending

Both theoretical and empirical development of the connection between gender equality and men's homicide are clearly needed. The work of Polk (1994a, 1994b) begins such examination using data from outside the United States. No similar studies of the connection between men's homicide offending and gender systems have been done in the United States.

A preliminary examination of U.S. data on men and homicide offending reveals there is some merit in considering men and gender in understanding men's homicide offending. To perform this examination, the same traditional, social, and economic equality variables applied to women's homicide were applied to men's rates of offending. The stepwise OLS regression procedure was done to reveal the best empirical model from the available variables examined. This procedure allows a determination of whether gender variables truly do provide substantive improvement over traditional explanations in understanding men's rates of homicide. Men's overall, intimate partner, family, and acquaintance homicides were analyzed.

*Men, gender, and homicide: the overall picture.* First, the overall picture of men's homicide offending rates is examined, as depicted in Table 5.1. In the men's overall homicide rate, a mixture of traditional and gender equality variables best explains the overall rates. This supports the theoretical argument that gender can be useful and appropriate in understanding men who kill and an addition to existing theory.

There is evidence that existing theory does contribute to explaining men's overall homicide offending. Population heterogeneity, population density, the percentage of those divorced or separated, and poverty are all significant and positive predictors of men's homicide rates, as traditional homicide theory predicts. Thus the effects of community disruption, instability, and potential conflict are still important considerations for understanding men who kill, despite any added benefit of gender variables. This connection between general community factors and men's homicide is consistent with the more public context of most men's homicide offending.

Although traditional explanations for homicide overall are important for explaining men's homicide offending, this analysis also shows the empirical importance of considering gender in men's

**Table 5.1    Model for Men's Total Homicide Offending Rates**

| Variable | Beta | p |
|---|---|---|
| Log of percentage African American | 0.461 | <0.001 |
| Log of population density | 0.136 | 0.016 |
| Percentage divorced or separated | 0.253 | <0.001 |
| Percentage of families in poverty | 0.338 | <0.001 |
| Gender equality in income | 0.162 | 0.005 |
| Rate of cohabiting couples per 100,000 | −0.243 | <0.001 |
| Percentage of male single-headed households | 0.178 | 0.008 |
| Population size (1990) | 0.053 | 0.230 |
| Log of percentage male 15–39 | 0.005 | 0.931 |
| Adjusted $R^2$ | 0.698 | |
| Significance of F ($R^2$) | <0.001 | |

offending. In this analysis both economic and social gender equality measures are important in explaining why men kill. As predicted, as the parity in income between men and women increases, men's overall homicide rates increase. In other words, in general men's homicide rate is higher when women make more money relative to men. What is important is that this measure is relative rather than absolute. It does not matter how many women are employed or how professional their employment is; what matters is whether their salaries equal those of men. What is telling about this variable and the symbolic threat involved in wage earning is that none of the cities in the sample had reached complete parity in men's and women's median incomes. Thus the threat of women's economic equality is more perceived than achieved, but that threat still has a significant impact on men's lethal violence.

Men's rates of homicide offending, like women's, decrease when cohabitation increases. The fact that cohabitation decreases men's overall homicide rates supports the contention that the release of both men and women from the traditional expectation that they should be in traditional marriages can benefit men's lives. This less traditional environment must create a context in which men are less likely to kill overall. One reason could be a reduced sense of entrapment and duty, which can be represented by traditional marriage, or an increased sense of social equality with women and a lower normative expectation or acceptance of men's control. This indicator may also serve as a proxy for a more general nontraditionalism that may help men avoid homicide offending.

The measure of single parenting also was significant in men's overall homicide offending, demonstrating a negative outcome for more egalitarian sharing of child rearing in single-parent homes. Analysis of men's overall homicide rates revealed that the greater the percentage of single-parent households headed by men, the greater the rate of men's overall homicide offending. This finding is contrary to the notion that fewer social restrictions on women will help men. This indicator specifically addresses child-rearing expectations. Men's rates of lethal violence appear to be negatively impacted when men represent a more proportional share of heads of single households with children. The beneficial effect of an increase in men's sharing such responsibilities appears to apply only to women. Perhaps the negative impact of single-headed households lies in the stress of child rearing and not in the lack of acceptability of men as child caregivers. Further investigation is clearly needed to better understand this finding.

*Men, gender, and homicide offending: the case of intimate partners.* The usefulness of gender equality predictors seen with overall men's rates is not found in an initial analysis of men's intimate partner homicide offending rates. Instead, the variables associated with the traditional concepts of heterogeneity, familial instability, and poverty are the best predictors of men's rates of intimate killing. The strongest influences observed here on the rate men kill intimate partners are those that generally affect community. This does not necessarily mean gender is not applicable but, rather, that the exploratory analysis conducted did not reveal significant regression coefficients.

Although gender equality variables used in Table 5.2 were not successful, these findings do not preclude gendered explanations of why these variables are important. The relationship between lethal violence and spousal estrangement may incorporate several gender-based dimensions. This relationship may be a function of how acceptable it is and how many attempts are made to control women in ending relationships. Additionally, the connection between poverty and men's intimate homicide offending can be interpreted from a gender standpoint. Hegemonic masculinity expectations include an emphasis on work, pay, and economic success. The value and expectation of men's self-sufficiency and the emasculation provided by poverty can make sense out of the strong influence on men's intimate partner offending. A greater influence of poverty can have a negative

**Table 5.2    Model for Men's Intimate Partner Homicide Offending Rates**

| Variable | Beta | p |
|---|---|---|
| Log of percentage African American | 0.275 | 0.001 |
| Percentage divorced or separated | 0.159 | 0.040 |
| Percentage of families in poverty | 0.192 | 0.019 |
| Population size (1990) | 0.118 | 0.076 |
| Log of percentage male 15–39 | –0.093 | 0.174 |
| Adjusted $R^2$ | 0.253 | |
| Significance of F ($R^2$) | <0.001 | |

impact on men's culture in that whereas expectations for making money do not decrease, the means by which to do so seem less reachable. The effect becomes a more general one on the larger social ethos that affects individual men in their daily lives. These theorized connections between poverty and men's homicide are related to gender and indirectly to gender equality, but they cannot be successfully modeled at the macro level using the measures available for this analysis.

Also notable is the relative inadequacy of traditional variables included to explain men's rates of killing intimate partners, which demonstrates that something is missing from traditional homicide's explanations of men's intimate partner homicides. Given the difficulty in operationalizing gender equality and the limits on those variables, gender equality as an explanation for this kind of homicide needs closer examination. Given the general problem of explanation and the limitations of the gender variables included here, one cannot discount the potential for gender equality variables to help explain this type of men's homicide.

*Gender, men, and homicide: the killing of family members.* Gender also appears helpful in explaining men's rates of killing family members. In analysis of men's family homicide rates, social equality variables added to the explanatory power of traditional homicide variables. (See Table 5.3.)

Familial instability and poverty, as traditional predictors, significantly increased the rates of men's killing of family members. Thus men's family homicide rates behaved as would be expected from existing homicide theory. Population size, a control variable, signifi-

**Table 5.3    Model for Men's Family Homicide Offending Rates**

| Variable | Beta | p |
|---|---|---|
| Percentage divorced or separated | 0.440 | <0.001 |
| Percentage of families in poverty | 0.273 | <0.001 |
| Rate of cohabiting couples per 100,000 | −0.273 | <0.001 |
| Population size (1990) | 0.183 | 0.002 |
| Log of percentage male 15–39 | −0.028 | 0.673 |
| Adjusted $R^2$ | | 0.415 |
| Significance of F ($R^2$) | | <0.001 |

cantly increased men's killing of family members. These findings suggest that men respond to public, community characteristics in this domestic homicidal context.

One social equality variable was significant in this study of men who kill family members. As observed overall, higher rates of cohabitation were a factor in decreasing the men's family homicide rate. This suggests that nontraditional intimate relationships help to protect men from lethally violent situations involving family members. The family homicide rate is composed of homicides against family members other than the spouse or other intimate partner. If we focus on the portion of this rate that includes infants and children, it could be argued that the culture of cohabitation can benefit the general family environment. Extended more broadly, release from the demands of traditional marriage could decrease stresses experienced with traditional marriage and children. As a more general proxy for social equality, the cohabitation rate could also suggest that more flexibility in gender roles and fewer traditional pressures can help keep men away from situations in which family members are killed.

*Men, gender, and homicide: acquaintances.* Exploring gender equality and men's homicide offending would be incomplete without examining the largest category of men's homicide offenses: acquaintances. Acquaintances include all persons who are known to the offender but are not involved on a familial or intimate level. Barroom brawls, conflicts between neighbors, gang violence, and other such acts come to mind. The possible influence of gender equality on this sort of homicide, although it could be argued, is less clear.

To explore a possible effect of gender equality on men's acquaintance homicide, the same OLS stepwise analysis was done to see if any of the gender equality variables were found in the best explanation for men's killing of acquaintances. (See Table 5.4.)

This analysis shows that traditional explanations appear best suited for explaining men's killing of acquaintances. Heterogeneity and poverty, usual factors in men's homicide offending, also significantly increase rates of men's acquaintance homicide. As traditional theory predicts, community diversity (with its potential for conflict) and economic hardship increase the rate at which men kill acquaintances. Population size as a control variable significantly increases

**Table 5.4   Model for Men's Acquaintance Homicide Offending Rates**

| Variable | Beta | p |
|---|---|---|
| Log of percentage African American | 0.444 | <0.001 |
| Percentage of families in poverty | 0.404 | <0.001 |
| Population size (1990) | 0.085 | 0.099 |
| Log of percentage male 15–39 | –0.019 | 0.717 |
| Adjusted $R^2$ | | 0.554 |
| Significance of F ($R^2$) | | <0.001 |

the men's acquaintance offending rate. No gender equality variables remained as important predictors of men's rates of killing acquaintances. This is not surprising, as most acquaintance killings involve conflicts in public places—like bars and the streets—and men killing men. The measures of gender equality included were indicators of women's equality and opportunity best suited to those private spheres in which gender structures and expectations are more obviously played out in men's and women's interactions.

Although this analysis leaves doubt as to the direct effect of women's equality and opportunity on men's killing of acquaintances, such homicide can be seen as connected to public demonstrations of hegemonic masculinity (see Messerschmidt, 1993), which value control and dominance. The dynamics of such demonstrations in acquaintance homicide are only indirectly related to gender equality itself. The concept of hegemonic masculinity may not be amenable to macrolevel analysis with variables currently available. More in-depth, qualitative research may reveal the way gender plays out in these situations and give insight as to whether and how research might be able to quantify those gender influences on men, particularly with regard to men's acquaintance homicide offending.

The use of gender equality shows some promise for explaining men's overall and family killing rates. The concept is also applicable theoretically to men's killing of intimate partners, although the indicators used in this study are not sensitive enough to detect gender influences. Gender may also play a role in men's killing of acquaintances, but it is more removed from gender equality per se. The connection among gender, gender equality, and men's homicide offending rates must be explored further if we are to understand men's offending and homicide in general.

## Gender Equality and Men's Homicide Offending:
## The Need to Examine Diversity

It can be strongly argued that the impact of gender on men's homicide offending and men's lives in general is experienced through the cultural expectations and definitions of manhood. Hegemonic masculinity makes demands on men to be tough, dominant, financially successful, and heterosexually active (see, e.g., Connell, 1995; Messerschmidt, 1993). These demands can have a strong impact on men's willingness and likelihood to use lethal violence. Lethal gang turf wars, domestic homicide, and deadly hate crimes could all involve such masculinity considerations. The ways in which men demonstrate masculinity and are punished for not being "real men" may have a profound influence on the context of and willingness to use violence.

It is not enough, though, to suggest that gender and gender equality impact all men's lives in equal ways. Scholars such as Jeff Hearn (1998) and Hearn and David Collinson (1994) have argued that differences between men are important to consider in examining men and masculinities. Although all men share some common characteristics, including masculinity demands, examining different types of men is important for a full assessment of the intersections of manhood and homicide offending and how men may differ from each other in this way. Such areas as race and ethnicity, class, sexual orientation, and age are important. The demands of hegemonic masculinity can be experienced differently by men who are not upper middle class, white, and heterosexual.

Some extant work suggests that class may be an important source of differentiation that affects men's criminal activity. Messerschmidt's (1993) examination of the intersections of hegemonic masculinity and nonlethal crimes finds that men's experiences with and resources to meet the demands of hegemonic masculinity differ by class; the man on the factory floor, the man engaged in street life, and the man in upper management have very different experiences of manhood, which result in different patterns of deviant and criminal behavior. Class difference in violence can include everything from men's street violence to male-centered corporate acts that result in pain, suffering, and even death to others. It is difficult to see corporate violence as violence, however (see, e.g., Chapple, 1998). Thus not only men's patterns and contexts of violence but also their criminal definitions differ. The prosecution of corporate executives for assault and manslaughter is virtually unheard of, yet acts of some companies have resulted in more harm than street crime ever could.

Race and ethnicity is another dimension that affects the connection among men, gender, and homicide offending. Research shows that minority men, particularly African Americans and Latinos, are disproportionately represented among homicide offenders and victims. This observation strongly suggests that additional factors impact minority men that differ from their white counterparts. Researchers in the area of masculinities (e.g., Mac An Ghaill, 1994; Brod, 1994) have described the intersections of race and ethnicity and manhood. Some have begun to examine the connection of race and ethnicity and homicide offending (e.g., Block, 1993; Phillips, 1997; Neapolitan, 1998), although most of this work has not incorporated gender considerations that may shed light on some of the differences between majority and minority men and homicide offending.

Minority and immigrant men live in a society still prejudiced with regard to color and citizen status. Men of color experience manhood not only in terms of what is expected from all men but also within the specific experiences of their particular culture and within a racist society. Definitions of manhood and appropriate or expected behavior can differ by race and ethnicity with regard to men's relationships with women and with other men, response to the economic and cultural system of a prejudiced society, and other such areas. In other words, being a man may not always be the same for white men and men of color.

The impact of racism, discrimination, prejudice, stereotyping, and other negative and painful experiences of living in U.S. society can be powerful influences on young minority men and their cultural and economic resources for being men. For example, Hill-Collins (1991) describes one cause of domestic violence by African American men as a power-seeking response to the lack of power experienced outside the home in a racist society. Thus domestic homicides committed by African American men against their intimate partners could have a strong base in masculinity concerns within an emasculating society. Pierrett Hondagneu-Sotelo and Michael Messner (1994) link the ways Mexican immigrant men enact masculinity to their relative status of power, which differs from that of men in the white majority.

Another difference between majority and minority men's homicides may involve the gang context. Carolyn Block (1993), in her research in Chicago, found that most of the excess risk for Latino male homicide had to do with street gang–related homicides. Also, Latino and African American men differed in their homicide offending rates. Differences in power, prestige, protection, and the like between minority and white men and between different minorities are likely to have an impact on the situations and rationales for committing murder and deserve careful attention as we theorize and research men, gender, and homicide offending.

Gay and bisexual men are also worth examining in assessing the impact of diversity among men on gender and homicide. The traditional hegemonic ideals that comprise expectations of men include heterosexuality. Michael Kimmel (1994), for example, defines masculinity as homophobia and describes the ways in which gay and heterosexual men experience power and manhood differently in society. Richard Collier (1998) argues that men's sexuality and violence against both men and women are intricately connected. Gay and bisexual men are at greater risk for victimization from straight men because of some men's violent reaction to homosexuality. Matthew Shepard, a gay college student in Wyoming, was killed by heterosexuals who beat him viciously because he violated this traditional masculinity norm. Increased victimization may place gay and bisexual men at greater risk for homicide offending as a self-defensive measure.

Experiences of homophobia, discrimination, and other issues faced by gay and bisexual men can potentially have a great impact on the situations and rationales for homicide offending that differ from those of their heterosexual counterparts. A study of gender, men, and homicide cannot ignore the potential impact of sexuality.

Age also has an influence on men, violence, and homicide offending. Among juvenile homicide offenders, boys represent a much larger proportion than girls. Charles Patrick Ewing (1990) and Meda Chesney-Lind and Randall Shelden (1992) report that boys constitute more than 90 percent of juvenile homicide offenders. Furthermore, unlike the general trend in all adult and girl-perpetrated homicide offending, the rate for boys has not decreased appreciably since around 1980. Indeed, young males who kill have been a major focus of concern for society.

Juvenile boys are at a critical point in their development of identities as men and young adults. Adolescence is the time of learning in all areas of manhood including sexual and other intimate relationships, public relationships with other men, and development of self-image and self-respect. Violence can be used as a means to demonstrate a boy's development as a man in any of these areas, and it is a response that is more likely overall to occur during these years of psychosocial development than later in life.

An additional crucial dimension of the age-gender connection in the homicide offending of males is the gang and group context. Research in this area specifically with respect to gender has been scarce, but it stands to reason theoretically that masculinity concerns can play a strong role in gang behaviors, particularly those that involve defense of territory and honor. John Hagedorn (1998) concludes that understanding masculinity is critical for understanding gangs, including their violent behavior.

An observation made about juveniles who kill family members is that they are likely to have experienced familial abuse (e.g., Busch et al., 1990; Daly and Wilson, 1988). Abuse was found to be particularly relevant in cases of killing parents (e.g., Heide, 1992, 1999; Ewing, 1990, 1997). The abuser (and victim) was most often the father; murdered mothers were not typically abusive, although emotional abuse may have occurred (Daly and Wilson, 1988). Killing a parent is described as the final effort after many failed attempts to escape abuse. These findings apply to both boys and girls, although boys comprise a much larger proportion of the youth in these studies. The abuse-homicide connection described by Kathleen Heide and others strongly resembles some of the dynamics of battered women who kill. Thus we need to examine dimensions of power as they relate not only to men and women in the home but also to the power of adult men in the home and how it affects young boys.

Using gender to understand men and homicide offending is a theoretical and analytical approach that is only in the beginning stages. As this work gains momentum, it will be crucial to focus on diversity among men. Some of this research, particularly that which addresses race and ethnicity, may be amenable to quantitative analysis of available homicide data. Other, more qualitative methods will likely be needed to examine the experience of masculinity and homicide offending among diverse groups of men, especially in research-

ing class, sexual orientation, and other kinds of diversity not recorded in official statistics.

## Intersections of Diversity
## and Women's Homicide Offending

We also need to expand research and theory into the area of diversity
in women's homicide offending. To presume that all women experience life in the same way is shortsighted. Gender equality has affected women differently according to race and ethnicity, class, sexual
orientation, and other such dimensions. Diversity among women and
their experiences with gender equality are crucial to a full examination of the linkages between gender equality and women's homicide
offending.

One important element of diversity that can impact women and
their relationships to gender equality and homicide is race and ethnicity. This is a relatively neglected area with respect to the
macrolevel effects of gender equality on women's homicide offending. Feminists of color (e.g., Hill-Collins, 1991; Davis, 1981; hooks,
1984) have long criticized feminism and the feminist movement as
representing primarily middle-class white women's interests and
neglecting the lives of minority women. Race has been shown to be
critical in most areas of criminology and, as such, should not be
ignored in understanding women's homicide. The analysis presented
here used indicators and women's homicide rates that were not race
sensitive. Some methodological difficulties arise when women's
homicide rates are disaggregated by race (even defined as simply
white and nonwhite). This process results in very small numbers for
some types of homicide, which is problematic for statistical analyses
such as multiple regression. This, however, does not mean attempt-
ing to understand how women's homicide offending is impacted by
race is not important. It does mean that methodological problems
currently limit race and women's homicide offending to theoretical,
descriptive, and ethnographic discussion.

Women of color (usually defined as African American women)
are disproportionately represented among women homicide offenders, usually totaling nearly 90 percent of the total number (see
Chapter 1). For the 179 cities with populations over 100,000 in 1990
with complete homicide data, nonwhite women constituted 72.9 per-

cent of offenders who were women, when race of offender was known. The vast overrepresentation of women of color in these homicide statistics suggests that additional factors affect women of color that are not present for their white counterparts and are not reflected in most theorizing about and research on women's homicide offending rates.

Feminists of color (hooks, 1984; Davis, 1981; Hill-Collins, 1991) argue that the lives of minority women must be viewed with respect to the intersections of race, class, and gender. They argue that not only are women of color exposed to discrimination and oppression because of their gender, but they are also oppressed by racism and classism that make experiences of gender different from those of white women. In the African American experience, for example, oppression in terms of workplace equality by race is said to intensify the risk of violence in the home. African American women are penalized doubly in the workplace because they are women and they are minorities.

The connection between racism and the domestic violence of African American men also cannot be ignored (hooks, 1984). The struggles African Americans—men and women—face in a racist world are said to be brought home, particularly when they are denied power in the public sphere. According to Hill-Collins (1991), African American men seek to achieve the status of "master" as identified by white patriarchal society, and when they are "blocked from doing so can become dangerous to those closest to them" (186). Thus the effects of racism on nonwhite women directly and through the impact of racism on the nonwhite men in their lives must be taken into account. Generalized theorizing is not sensitive to race and gender intersections, and this study was unable to address them.

Macrolevel analysis of minority women and homicide offending rates carries many difficulties. First, further disaggregation of cases by race within gender creates several categories with very small numbers, thus making analyses such as regression too unstable. This occurs even when race is aggregated into the general category of nonwhite. Second, statistical analysis of behavior of minorities in a collapsed category such as nonwhite obscures any substantive differences that may exist between different types of nonwhites. This poses some theoretical problems. Although racism and oppression are leveled against anyone who is not part of the white power structure, the experience of oppression both from whites and from men may be very different for nonwhite women than for their white coun-terparts. It is difficult to imagine, for example, that the experience of discrimination and gender oppression would be the same for women of Asian and African American descent, although both are defined as minorities. Hill-Collins (1991) notes the image and expectation that African American women are strong and are able to take care of themselves. This image creates several problematic expectations for African American women, including encouraging the silence that accompanies abuse from men. Some traditional Asian cultures, on the other hand, may emphasize silence about domestic violence because of demands that wives be submissive to and dependent on their husbands. An understanding of homicide needs to include the experiences of all offenders regardless of gender, race, and class. Methodologically, the best approach to race and women's homicide is to pursue quantitative research and engage in qualitative research that gives those experiences visibility, so that theorizing can be more firmly grounded in the empirical reality of the lives of women of color.

Class also has an impact on the lives of women. Women in dif-ferent classes will likely experience gender equality and opportunity differently, and those differences could play out in homicide offend-ing. One area to consider is the effect class status has on men. Previous analysis demonstrated the importance of men's violence in understanding women's intimate partner homicide. Therefore, inas-much as class has an influence on men's violence, we could expect class to affect the situations that could result in women's homicide offending. This possibility seems even more likely when the strong poverty-homicide relationship in men's homicide offending is taken into account.

Class is also embedded in the equality measures used. Economic equality measures, found to be the most useful for understanding women's rates of intimate homicide, clearly would have a differen-tial impact by class. Women's employment rates were found to impact the rates of women's homicide offending, but the statistic of employment rate incorporates the assumption that employment is lib-erating. The degree to which employment may be liberating most likely is defined by class. Working-class women have been more strongly represented in the workforce and for a longer time than mid-dle- and upper-class women. This labor, however, has been concentrated in low-paying jobs that may not provide the kind of liberation expected for women, including those from more privileged classes.

Sexual orientation is another source of women's differences. Lesbians and bisexual women experience gender and gender equality in ways often different from other women; they may also experience victimization differently. Linda Bernhard (2000) found that lesbians were significantly more likely than heterosexual women to experience physical victimization in general. She postulated that some of the difference was related to hate crimes and street violence, although that was not directly examined. The lesbians in Bernhard's study were also significantly more likely than heterosexual women to do nothing about the violence.

Like gay and bisexual men, lesbian and bisexual women are at greater risk of victimization because of their sexuality. In addition to physical victimization, lesbian and bisexual women have been subjected to sexual victimization by men who insist that all homosexual women need is a "good man." Thus the strength of the deviant definition of women's homosexual behavior and the hegemonic masculine demand for men's demonstration of dominance and sexual prowess are linked to traditional gender norms represented in social equality. Lethal violence as a defensive action could be lessened for lesbians and bisexual women if social equality were high. This impact could be great for nonheterosexual women, given the intricate connections between traditionalism and situations that could elicit a lethal, self-defensive action.

An additional dimension of women's sexual orientation that can provide differences in women's experience is lesbian battering. Although very little work has been done on the subject, we know it does occur, although the typical image of a battered woman is not one of a lesbian victim. Bernhard (2000) found that several lesbian women in her study had suffered physical and verbal abuse from their sexual partners. Claire Renzetti (1998) argues that lesbian relationships are not the same as heterosexual women's relationships and that this difference must be taken into account in studying lesbian battering. She found that lesbians who are battered are less likely than heterosexuals to have access to services for battered women, which results in far fewer lesbian victims seeking help. She adds that the criminal justice system is very little help, with statutes in some states disallowing homosexuals from filing domestic violence charges. This could directly affect women's homicide offending, as a large number of women's homicides can be traced to self-defensive and conflict situations that have resulted from an escalation of abuse.

Although the issue of heterosexual women's domestic violence victimization has become more visible in scholarly and public awareness, lesbian battering is still neglected in program and policy considerations and has only recently been the subject of scholarly study (e.g., Renzetti, 1998). This invisibility can result in lesbian battering escalating more greatly than heterosexual battering before coming to the attention of criminal justice agencies who may or may not take the violence seriously. Agencies devoted to assisting battering victims are less likely to offer services or be sensitive to lesbians and may be of little help. Clearly, the experiences of lesbian and bisexual women in a homophobic society can have a strong impact on the relationship among women, equality, and homicide.

Age also has a direct impact on the context of homicide offending by women. Adolescent and preadolescent girls, like their adult counterparts, represent a very small proportion of youthful homicide offenders (Ewing, 1990; Chesney-Lind and Shelden, 1992). Girls, also like their adult counterparts, are more likely than boys to kill family members and are very unlikely to kill in the context of another crime. Another difference lies in the number of girls' victims that are infants, very often children of unwed mothers (Ewing, 1990). Girls engage in homicidal acts that are often related to neglect and abuse, usually by parents (Ewing, 1990; Russell, 1985; Heide, 1992). Because of their age and gender, girls are vulnerable to victimization by family members. The act of homicide in this context is usually a last-resort effort to end physical, sexual, or emotional abuse by a parent.

Although this action is similar to the self-defensive actions of a battered intimate partner, the juvenile girl faces a juvenile justice and welfare system that officially criminalizes girls' attempts to escape abuse. Running away, violating curfew, and committing other such status offenses result in the girl being returned to the home or detained in a juvenile institution (known for their abuse as well; Chesney-Lind, 1989). For some, a gender-insensitive system may create the view that lethal violence is the only way out. The effects of social equality in this situation directly relate to the value placed on girls' abuse claims and the amount of resources to deal with that abuse. Low social equality would more likely result in a system characterized by a strong emphasis on traditional gender norms and the punishing of girls who violated those norms by complaining or otherwise causing problems. It is clear that age has a demonstrative effect on the qualitative, if not quantitative, difference in the gender equality and homicide connection for girls versus adult women.

Similarly, we can hypothesize that older women would experience differences in the way gender equality and opportunity play out in their lives, which would be pertinent for understanding age differences in women's homicide offending. Clearly, contexts differ between adults and adolescents-preadolescents, and these contexts need to be fully explored in examinations of gender equality and homicide offending.

Consideration of diversity among women is a crucial step for elucidating the connections between gender structures and relations and the commission of homicides by women. Further research is needed, qualitative and quantitative where possible, to give the fullest picture of how levels of equality and opportunity can affect women's lives and their likelihood of becoming murderers.

U.S. society is characterized by varying degrees of gender equality and opportunity, although nowhere have we reached the point where gender does not result in different structural opportunities and cultural expectations for men and women. Such a pervasive system as gender must therefore play into the patterns and situations that result in homicide. This study demonstrates the utility of examining gender equality and women homicide offenders as an overall group.

The gender system may also have a demonstrable effect on men who kill, even above and beyond our traditional male-centered theories of homicide. Despite recent declines in homicides by men, far too many deaths occur at the hands of men for us not to carefully examine all influence on men's lives that can affect lethal violence. Hegemonic masculine ideals cannot be ignored in explaining men's homicide offending, and the interrelationships of men and women make the concept of equality and opportunity for women part of a valid research agenda for understanding men who kill. Preliminary theoretical application and data analysis support the call for more gender-based research on men's homicide.

Finally, extending the application of gender equality to homicide offending needs to include the ways men and women interact within the gender system—not only through their gender but in terms of their race and ethnicity, class, sexual orientation, age, and other factors. We cannot understand how gender and homicide are connected without exploring the multiple ways that connection is experienced by diverse persons. Theory and research addressing the gender system and homicide offending need to incorporate those differences.

# 6

## Conclusion: Directions in Women's Homicide

This study has shed light on the connection between gender equality and women's homicide offending rates, but several questions and areas for further consideration of women's lethal violence remain. First, the importance of the homicide context and women offenders needs further discussion, particularly with respect to how women's lives affect the context in which they kill. Second, it is necessary to address theory building with regard to homicides committed by women, including not just the complexities of including gender systems but also factors other than gender equality. By including both gender and nongender variables, researchers can take steps toward developing a complete theoretical model for women's homicide offending.

Third, research on women who kill needs to further address data and method limitations. Finally, it is necessary to contemplate directions for future research on women who kill and the policy and practice implications of what we know about women homicide offenders. The empirical research presented here provides support for gender-centered policy that would improve the lives of all and facilitate a decreased risk of lethal violence by women.

### Understanding Women Who Kill

As we have seen, women's homicide offending can serve as an indicator of the quality of women's lives, because women's rates of killing decrease as women's lives improve. The goal of explaining women's homicide offending raises several concerns regarding both theory building and methodology in such offending.

## The Importance of Context

One of the most important considerations in building women's homicide explanations is the diverse contexts in which the homicidal action takes place. Disaggregating homicide rates by victim-offender relationship reveals that homicides are not all the same and that homicide as a phenomenon is not unidimensional. Kirk Williams and Robert Flewelling (1988) and Robert Parker and Allison Toth (1990), for example, demonstrate the value of disaggregating the overall homicide rate. This study affirms the great importance of disaggregation in showing how and where men and women differ in rates of killings and the differences in homicides committed by women. Each victim-offender context has unique characteristics.

One key distinction in victim-offender relationships involves public and private domains. Homicides in the public sphere include those of acquaintances and strangers. The public sphere includes the criminal subculture, street culture, workplace culture, and other arenas of public life that are more visible and that are composed of relationships that may include criminal enterprise or interactions that regularly take place in view of others (such as friends and coworkers). This sphere is much more susceptible to the disorganization of community, which decreases a community's internal controls to regulate public life. This sphere is also influenced by the dramaturgy of public space (see, e.g., Campbell, 1986; Messerschmidt, 1993) and the notions of gaining territory, demonstrating dominance, and achieving public recognition of self-worth. Men have traditionally dominated this arena, and it is in this arena that men tend to commit a greater share of homicides.

The law of self-defense incorporates the assumption that the situations that lead to lethal violence are typically those of the bar brawl that gets out of hand or the murderous stranger hiding in the bushes (Gillespie, 1989). These images reflect public-sphere relationships in which interaction is intermittent, brief, and voluntary. Thus it is no surprise that public-sphere homicides for men and women, as represented in acquaintance homicide rates, are fairly well explained by existing explanations that are more sensitive to these characteristics. Traditional explanations may be less useful for women's homicide because women are less likely to interact in the public sphere.

The private sphere entails a set of relationships that have very different characteristics. As Richard Gelles (1993, 1997) discusses, the family as a social group is characterized by several unique features including interactions that are lengthy, intense, private, involuntary, and that include a right to influence, among others. These features create a different character for private-sphere relationships. In one sense these relationships are isolated and secluded from the world, as has been the case legally and idealistically (i.e., the home as a "haven" from the world). In another sense, relationships are much more susceptible to stresses less likely to be perceived as escapable.

The influences of macrolevel indicators on private-sphere relationships are much more indirect than they are in the public sphere. The influence occurs through the public-sphere conditions that affect stresses and beliefs that are taken into the home and that regulate the public interaction of those in the home. At the same time, several factors influence domestic relationships that have not been modeled in traditional homicide theory: these include normative systems around gender roles, child rearing and other caregiving, and government and other assistance to families, to name a few. The analysis in this study shows that attempts to model some of these other factors are fruitful and necessary for understanding homicide in the private sphere. The relative failure of traditional predictors to explain much of the variance in men's domestic homicide offending lends credibility to the significance of the division between these spheres outside of gender concerns. It also indicates that the type of relationship between perpetrator and victim, in addition to gender considerations, is crucial for a fuller picture of homicide offending.

## Dimensions of Patriarchy and Women's Homicide Offending

In expanding our understanding of women who kill, it is necessary to explore the complexity of a patriarchal gender system and what it means for women. Gender equality in this study was measured in both economic and social terms. Economic equality showed less of an effect overall to decrease women's homicide offending rates when compared to the power of social equality. Several observations can be made with regard to the relationship between social and economic dimensions of patriarchy. In the early days of the women's movement and public concern for women's status, a focus was placed on wage earning and right to work. Emphasis was given to breaking down the "glass ceilings" and barriers to women's equal employment opportunities and wages through legislation, awareness, and collective demand for equal rights. Subsequently, society saw the passage and enforcement of equal opportunity legislation at the state and federal levels. Although many (e.g., England and Browne, 1992) have found women's poverty to have increased, proportionally, gains have been made in women's pay and levels of workforce participation. In several cities in the sample, for example, a greater proportion of women were working than men. Thus economics of difference are slowly improving in some areas. This may account in part for the less than significant overall individual influence of economic gender equality observed.

Changes in meaning and normative systems around gender, as evidenced by social equality, have come much more slowly. As Max Weber observed, ideas change much more slowly than structures. This is evidenced in the persistence of the importance of social equality indicators in explaining women's homicide rates, regardless of the victim-offender context examined. Women's homicide offending rates were affected less by structural economic opportunities and affected more by traditional normative structures that encourage situations that make lethal violence more likely. These structures include the legal and traditional institution of marriage and expectations for caregiving, as measured by low scores on the proportion of men who are single parents. The role of women's status as divorced or separated is too complicated methodologically to examine at the macro level, but theoretically it still follows that higher numbers of divorced or separated women would indicate fewer normative restrictions on women to be in official marriages and more freedom to live as singles.

In summary, with regard to gender equality and homicide rates this analysis of 1990 data indicates that the negative impact of low gender equality may have shifted from objective opportunity and participation in the economic sphere to the somewhat less tangible expectations society has of women. The problems of low economic equality should not be ignored, however, as women's employment still decreases the rate at which women kill intimate partners. Women still need the financial means to have independence and freedom.

The relationship between the social and economic dimensions of gender equality with respect to women's homicide offending can merely be theorized at this point. Low gender equality and opportunity does not only consist of economic and social disadvantage for women. The impact of education, politics, and the legal system must be incorporated into a fuller understanding of how gender equality impacts women's risk of lethal violence. Attempts were made to incorporate data to address this issue, but available indicators were inadequate to capture the possible impact of other structural gender effects on women's homicide offending rates. More work needs to be done to further develop an empirical picture of the gender equality structure and its specific role in increasing women's lethal violence.

### Assessing Factors Other than Gender Equality in Women's Homicide Offending

Despite the improvements gender equality variables make in explaining women's (and men's) homicide offending rates, several variables from more traditional homicide models remain as key indicators of those rates. It is crucial to examine these factors to gain a more holistic view of homicide and the most complete modeling possible.

In examining traditional models of homicide between men and women, standard explanations differ in their ability to account for homicide offending rates. Some remaining factors, however, have an impact on men's and women's homicide offending and need a full accounting in any theoretical model building for women's homicide offending.

Poverty, for example, was an important variable for women's homicide offending rates, except in the killing of family members. Although empirically poverty appears important to both genders, significant differences are seen in the impact of poverty on men's and women's homicide rates for all categories except intimate partner killing. This indicates that although poverty affects both genders, it affects men more strongly. Theory and additional empirical research need to address the connection between the structures and cultures of poverty in urban areas and men's and women's lives to further sort out commonalities and differences. Other traditional variables useful for predicting women's homicide in some contexts were the percentage of African Americans and the percentage of those divorced or separated. The same questions apply here as they do for poverty.

Explaining significant traditional factors that operate in ways opposite from theoretical prediction is also an important component in a return to nongendered models of homicide offending. Population density had the opposite effect of that predicted in explaining women's overall and intimate partner homicide offending rates. The research of Joyce Nielson and colleagues (1992), Ola Barnett and colleagues (1997), and Gelles (1993, 1997) demonstrates that battered women experience isolation from the outside world. This isolation could be indicated by greater numbers of homicides committed in less dense areas with more physical space in which to be separated from others. Although the negative effects of population density could indicate this kind of isolation effect, the effect of population density on women's homicide offending rates needs more clarification. Additionally, analysis incorporating less urban areas needs to be done to further elucidate the population density–women's homicide relationship. There are points of compatibility at which traditional predictors help to explain women's as well as men's homicide offending rates. More research is needed to sort out areas of similarity and difference in common indicators of men's and women's rates. Furthermore, more data are needed on how poverty, family instability, heterogeneity, and other useful traditional indicators actually work in women's lives.

We must look specifically at the commonalities between men and women in intimate partner homicide offending and the interrelationship of men's and women's lethal violence against partners. As Table 3.8 (Chapter 3) shows, we cannot consider the factors affecting women's killing of partners without looking at violence committed against women. In fact, many traditional predictors cease to be significant when men's violence against women is included. This suggests that men's violence against women is an intervening factor between the social and ecological conditions of the city and women's rates of killing intimates. The remaining effects of population density on decreasing women's lethal violence and poverty on increasing it suggest a much more complex model of women's homicide offending that incorporates men's intimate violence.

## Data and Methodological Limitations

Research on women homicide offenders at the macroanalytical level requires attention to data and methodology limitations on several levels. First, women's homicide offending analysis is restricted by available data on homicide, as is all research of this type. A second problem has to do with the measurement and availability of standard homicide variables, which plagues other homicide research as well. Finally, although gender equality and opportunity need to be included in analyses of women's homicide offending, finding the applicable indicators that reflect the complexity of the patriarchal gender system is difficult.

### Limitations of Homicide Data

Homicide research and theory is hindered by methodological and data problems. Sources for homicide offending data are severely limited. Although mortality data from vital statistics and public health organizations provide additional sources for homicide victimization, macrolevel homicide offending data are limited to data from criminal justice sources. Reliability and validity, measurement, and causal specification issues continue to be problematic in the research of homicide and the development of empirically based theory.

This study employed Supplementary Homicide Reports data, gathered as part of the FBI's Uniform Crime Reporting program. The reliability and validity of these data are dependent on the classification and reporting procedures used by law enforcement agencies. Although the quality of the SHR has improved over the years, missing information plagues the data. One can employ statistical weighting and adjusting procedures (such as those outlined in Williams and Flewelling, 1987) to approximate missing data, as this study did, but that is not a perfect solution. Moreover, as these data reflect homicides known to police and include known information about the perpetrators, there is much room for classification error. These are the only data, however, that allow for analysis of gender, homicide perpetration, and victim-offender relationship across the nation. The UCR reports arrest clearance rates for homicide by gender, but these data are not categorized using any other characteristics. Furthermore, arrest clearance data reflect more upon the policing and arrest practices of jurisdictions and provide yet another source of bias. Another alternative, researcher-collected data (e.g., as done by Mann, 1996), is limited in the number of jurisdictions from which data can be obtained and is plagued by recording biases that occur in individual departments. Therefore SHR data are the best for studying macrolevel homicide offending by gender, but they are plagued by problems that need to be continually acknowledged and compensated for (e.g., weighting and adjusting for missing data).

Another difficulty with SHR and other official data on homicide offending is the statistical difficulty of working with data on women. The numbers of homicides per city and even per state committed by women are often very small, which has undesirable effects on rate calculations that are overly sensitive to relatively small differences and can fluctuate a great deal over different periods of time. This study could not escape this source of error, and it is important to keep in mind that the primary goal of this research was to conduct a preliminary examination of how quantitative research on gender equality and women's homicide offending rates can be approached.

Further disaggregation of women's homicides by race-ethnicity and victim-offender relationship increases the amount of this error in analysis as the numbers of applicable homicides per category become too small to sustain meaningful multivariate, causal analysis. Thus although a full understanding of women homicide offenders requires attention to diversity among women, available macrolevel homicide data for women allow us to do little in this way. We are, then, continuing to face blurred distinctions among women in our analytical attempts to aggregate women homicide offenders. Any examination that provides insight into women who kill and that supports policies to improve women's lives, however, is worth doing despite these data weaknesses.

The proper level of analysis is a continuing problem in homicide research. Cities were chosen for this study because they reflect the unit of analysis that has the greatest potential to vary and thus to better test independent measures. There are problems with using cities, however. One, observable in these analyses, is the fact that the smaller the unit of analysis, the greater the potential for outlying and atypical cases, particularly when a phenomenon as variable as women's homicides is analyzed. Cities are no exception. In 1990 Corpus Christi had a high homicide rate for women, which had some impact on the analysis. New York City, as a very large city with some very extreme values on some of the indicators, also shows overall influence on such analyses.

City-level analysis also has advantages. The biggest advantage of using cities and units of analysis smaller than states is that the variability of homicides within the state can be exposed and examined. In California, for example, gender equality and the homicide rate varies greatly by city. Smaller units of analysis can help us pinpoint more precisely the effects of our indicators.

### Limitations of Independent Variable Measures

Cities also create problems in the availability of independent measures and with missing data. Whereas legislation and state political composition was used in the state-level work of Sugarman and Straus (1988) and Kersti Yllo (1983), no counterparts for these types of variables exist at the city level. Because of the paucity of city-level indicators, the comprehensive indexes created by Yllo and Sugarman and Straus cannot be developed. Instead, we can only use crude, individual-level indicators when doing macroanalytical analysis of urban homicide. Official data from such sources as the census provide most of these indicators. The problem with using these data, in addition to their inherent weaknesses, is the poor availability of indicators that reflect our theories.

*Traditional theoretical indicators.* The difficulties with traditional theoretical variables extend back to the beginning of such homicide research and continue to this day. Problems with data include the relative paucity of alternative measures for many variables, the high correlations between them (multicollinearity), and the validity of these measurements of independent variables for accurately representing the theoretical constructs they are drawn from. Others have more thoroughly addressed such issues (see, e.g., Land, McCall, and Cohen, 1990), but some questions will be considered here that arise from using secondary data for indicators of traditional theories of homicide.

Heterogeneity poses a problem in terms of both actual measurement and validity. What is an adequate measure of heterogeneity? Traditionally, the percentage of African Americans has been used, as it was in this study. This has generally been the case because of the relative size of this population and the high visibility of conflict with Anglo Americans. However, the assumption that an increase in African Americans reflects a heterogeneous population is too simplistic. There is a need for valid measures of other groups, particularly Latinos.[1] The U.S. Census measures the numbers who fit into their classification of Hispanic, but they are reported as white ethnicities. Furthermore, census data do not allow for an examination of the immigrant status of other ethnic groups in U.S. cities, particularly those from Europe and the Middle East. Thus available data make the actual measurement of heterogeneity imperfect and potentially flawed.

In addition to the problems encountered in composing the measure, we also must ask how valid the measure is in reflecting the community breakdown theorized to result from heterogeneity in race and ethnicity. Does a mix of white Anglo Americans and nonwhites mean a breakdown of community will occur? Across cities, we find several examples of ways heterogeneity does not represent community breakdown.

The available data on poverty also raise questions about how good our measurements are and how valid they are in representing poverty. These measures are drawn predominantly from census data but raise several questions. Do we measure poverty by using the percentage of families in poverty or of persons in poverty? When researching women, do we use poverty in general or women's poverty? Is women's poverty best measured by the percentage of female-headed households below the poverty line? Should households be included only if they have children, or should all women's households be included? Whose children are included—hers or all children in the household? Although the theory described here can assist us in these choices, the relative lack of alternative sources of poverty data leave few options, which may or may not be suited for our theoretical needs for studying women and homicide offending.

Another source of concern is the validity of poverty measures for theoretical constructs. Does the census-defined poverty line reflect people's reality of being poor? The stated income division does not represent the same cost of living from city to city. Living in Los Angeles or New York is much more expensive than living in Oklahoma City, Omaha, or Des Moines. There is a lack of ability to account for the internal variation in the experience of poverty, which challenges the validity of any poverty measure. Using Gini coefficients to measure relative deprivation between residents of cities assists us somewhat, but it cannot deal with the conceptual definitions of absolute deprivation.

Similarly, the other traditional predictors are usually limited to one or two official sources that cannot accommodate some of the specific theoretical needs of homicide research. Furthermore, these factors cannot be specifically applied to women. Researchers are then left with data that do not address the gender-specific effects of traditional community variables. In secondary research, social scientists are often constrained by such limitations and in the end must do the best with the available measures and triangulate measures when possible.

*Measuring gender equality and opportunity.* The measurement of gender equality poses even more challenges for those researching women and homicide. Economic equality is best measured by available secondary data, but it also faces several limitations. Most available secondary data for economic equality come from the census. Beyond the variables included in the analysis in this book, there are few other choices to represent women's economic status. Thus at the macroanalytical level, what is left is employment, parity with men in wages and employment, poverty, and participation in nontraditional women's occupations. These areas are more representative of a conceptual definition of equality with regard to economics than we find with other gender equality measures, but they are limited in their sensitivity to different facets of work, wages, and diversity that would help us to understand women who kill.

Social equality is much more difficult to analyze. No established measures define gender role segregation or gender normative systems. The U.S. Census does not directly incorporate these issues of social gender equality in its data collection, and no comparable data sources cover so many locations and levels of analysis. Thus this research must use very indirect measures that can serve as proxies for the dimension of social equality. Cohabitation and men's heading of single-parent households can theoretically represent some elements of gender normative systems, but until there is a direct accounting for and measurement of social expectations and roles as divided by gender, it is extremely difficult to examine social gender equality comprehensively.

This study used measures that represented only two dimensions of gender equality and opportunity: economic and social. Although legal equality has been studied in some state-level research (e.g., Baron, 1993), it cannot be examined at the city level because of the structure of law. Rates of domestic violence prosecution, arrest rates for domestic violence (not available through the UCR program), and other criminal justice measures could serve as some indicators of the treatment of women and women's issues by the legal system at the city level, if they could be obtained. Law pertinent to these anlyses is found only at the state and national level and can only be meaningfully incorporated at that level.

Measuring political equality is also affected by problems with city-level data. When cities are used as the units of analysis, there is a greater ability to account for intercity variation and apply the variables that are most appropriate at the community level. Unfortunately, no adequate available data encompass political representation vis-à-vis men at the city level. This study attempted unsuccessfully to incorporate such variables as the presence of a woman mayor. Studying the number of women in state legislatures and the U.S. Congress is also not revealing, as most cities have just one representative to the state legislature, and that person is often shared with other communities and rural areas. Representatives to the national government represent an even larger area. The best measure would be the proportion of women involved in city-level decisionmaking, but such data have not been compiled in any usable form. Additionally, there are questions of validity as not all cities have equal power vested in mayors or city councils, which makes the quantification of power virtually impossible. In other words, a large number of women on a city council in which the power is vested elsewhere means much less than a smaller but much more influential number of women who are in city councils that have greater power.

The evidence presented in this study shows that even highly imperfect measures hold value in analyzing women's homicide offending rates. It also suggests how great the potential is for explaining women who kill if better measures of gender equality and opportunity were available.

## Testing Causal Linkages

Another difficulty in homicide research and theory is the lack of specification achieved in theorizing the causal links between indicators and homicide. A discussion of the traditional predictors necessarily raises this problem. The subculture of violence, for example, is one theory that is prone to causal link issues. What does the observable relationship between the percentage of African Americans and nonwhites and the homicide rate mean? Subculture of violence theorists argue the intermediary link is the presence of a normative system of values and expectations that condone violence. With macrolevel analysis, however, this connection cannot be specified and thus must be assumed. This assumption, rampant in some areas of homicide study, is potentially biased and rarely examined.

Liqun Cao and colleagues (1997), in examining the belief systems of individuals, found that white males were slightly *more* likely than African American males to espouse a belief in violence. This is not the only theory or indicator with this problem; it extends to gender equality measures as well. What exactly is it about women's employment that helps decrease women's general risk of killing intimates? It is theorized that female employment reflects an opportunity structure to escape domestic violence, but such connections are theoretical and impossible to examine at the macro level. Clearly, more work is needed to link structural-level analysis with contextual-level data to further explain how gender and other structures actually operate to create a homicidal event.

## Directions for Future Research and Application

From this initial empirical and theoretical examination, it is clear that there are many directions the investigation of women's homicide offending can go, including the search for better theories about why women kill and better measurements of theoretical variables. Additional directions include the policy and practice implications for work within communities for what we already have discovered about the intersections of gender, women, and lethal violence.

### Empirical Questions

Theorizing about women's homicide and homicide in general must be empirically grounded and must include as much evidence as possible for specific causal links. Ideally, to accomplish this task involves a marriage of macro- and microlevel methods. The research presented here establishes a link between the lack of gender equality and homicide offending. The next step is to further explore how these links operate in the lives of those who kill. Angela Browne's (1987) work offers an excellent example of qualitative work that has helped make sense of the abuse-offending connection for abused women. More work needs to be done to examine how issues of poverty, heterogeneity, and gender experiences impact the lives of women who kill and how they might differ among types of homicide. Qualitative research can also help to elucidate differences among women who kill that cannot be modeled statistically in macrolevel analysis. These investigations are necessary to reveal the multidimensional nature of women's homicide offending.

## Policy and Practice Implications

Assessments of policy and practice implications are critical for any research. Research that is useful to society can help to improve the conditions in which we live. This is certainly true in the case of crime and homicide research in which theory and research give clues on how to address such criminal problems. This study provides direct suggestions as to how we can improve women's lives and decrease their likelihood to use lethal violence. Two primary implications for policy and programs emerge from this study.

The first implication informs policies and programs in the area of economics. The research findings underscore the importance of economically empowering women in society. Although economic equality was not a factor in many of the equations, there is still evidence of the importance of women's employment as a protective factor against women killing intimate partners. This clearly suggests that current and future efforts to continue to improve women's participation and support in the workforce are not misguided. The favorable impact of women's employment on decreasing women's homicide offending rates is only one indication that improved employment results in a general improvement in women's and potential victims' lives. Continued and improved enforcement of current equal employment and equal pay legislation is definitely needed. Additionally, other assistance that helps women in the workplace, such as child care and protection against other discrimination, can go a long way to empower and improve women's lives and, subsequently, help lower the rate of women's killing of intimate partners.

The second implication from this study is the necessity of continuing and instigating policies and programs that directly address social equality through the norms and expectations associated with gender. Education programs that confront long-held beliefs about domestic violence and other violence against women attack traditional beliefs about men's dominance and decrease the legitimacy of violence against women. Likewise, breaking down gender stereotypes among men is likely to result in less acceptance of violence as a means of demonstrating manhood. Education and other support for changing ideas will help improve the lives of women and men and decrease the use of lethal violence. Legislation, such as the federal Violence Against Women Act of 1994 and similar state-level initiatives, serves to criminalize men's violence against women and reinforce the value of women's lives and their right to be free from men's abusive dominance. Mandatory arrest policies and criminal justice policy changes like these can serve the same purpose. Such legislative and law enforcement examples will be likely to encourage the changing of thinking about traditional gender expectations in general, at least as they relate to domestic violence.

Women's homicide offending rates are clearly a function of both traditional theory and gender equality forces. The best explanations of women's homicide rates depend on the relational context between victim and offender, but all involve some combination of these two types of factors. Further research needs to examine additional dimensions of gender equality and its impact by race and for men. Additionally, qualitative research needs to examine the context of offending. This will help us identify more clearly the causal connections between the structural conditions that impact homicide and the way those conditions translate into action.

Relatively few women commit homicide, but women still kill more than a thousand victims each year. Victims' families are not the only ones who suffer when a woman commits homicide; families are torn apart when a woman goes to prison. This is especially true for the majority of offenders who leave children behind. The extended family and the foster care system usually fill the void left by the imprisoned mother. Thus for every victim and every woman offender, a larger social web also suffers because of the murder.

As long as society ignores women who kill, society also suffers because attention to improving women's equality benefits all of society. Continued research on women's homicide is important not only to make this lesser-known offending more visible but to support and encourage efforts of society to improve the lives of women and men in the hope of decreasing women's lethal violence and improving society as a whole.

## Note

1. I use *Latino*, acknowledging that the wide diversity of cultures within the Spanish-speaking peoples of the Americas is not fully represented.

# APPENDIX A:
# DATA AND METHODOLOGY

This appendix describes in detail the data and methods employed in this study of gender and women's homicide offending.

## Data: Dependent Variables

Data on homicide offending are drawn from the 1990 Supplementary Homicide Reports (SHR). The SHR is a part of the FBI's annual Uniform Crime Reports (UCR) program and gives information on homicides known to the police. Incidents may or may not end in arrest, and an arrest does not have to occur for a homicide to be included in these data. Four types of data are available: agency, incident, victim, and offender data. Offender data are used in this study; they include demographic information on race, age, and gender, as well as relationship between offender and victim, circumstances of the offense, and type of weapon used.

Homicides entail all cases of murder and nonnegligent manslaughter offending included in the Supplementary Homicide Reports for the 200 cities and Census Designated Places with a census-listed population of 100,000 or more. After excluding cities not reporting homicide to the SHR in 1990, 179 cities remained in the sample.[1]

Homicide offending rates were calculated for each gender and for the victim-offender relationship category. The latter refers to the relational context in which the killing occurred, including stranger, acquaintance, family member, and intimate partner. Stranger homicides were classified as those offenses involving parties that had no prior relationship. Intimate partners included offenders who were married, had been married, were living in common-law relationships, or had otherwise been sexually intimate with their victims. Family included those offenders who were related to but not intimately involved with their victims. Acquaintances included all others who had known their victim previously but were not intimately involved or related.

Rates were calculated using incidents for 1990 for cities that provided data. Incidences were weighted and adjusted according to the procedure described by Kirk Williams and Robert Flewelling (1987) to compensate for missing SHR data.[2] Incidences of homicides for cities by gender of offender and by offender relationship to victim were then used to calculate rates by dividing the incidences for men's or women's homicide offenses by the population of men or women in the city. This figure was then multiplied by 100,000 to create the rate per 100,000 population. Because of heavily skewed distributions, all homicide rates were transformed into natural logs for the analysis.

Weaknesses of the Supplementary Homicide Reports include lack of reporting of homicides and inaccurate or missing information about homicides known to reporting agencies (Tannenbaum, 1993). Additionally, Michael Maxfield (1989) has criticized SHR data for errors in the classification process surrounding the homicide circumstances that overestimate conflict homicides and underestimate instrumental homicides. Although the adjusting and weighting procedure used for these data attempts to compensate mathematically for missing data by victim-offender relationship, bias still likely exists in women's homicide offending rates, particularly for acquaintance homicide. On one hand, acquaintance homicides reflective of instrumental motives will likely be underestimated; on the other hand, classification procedures rely on available information. Thus many acquaintance homicides by women may actually be those committed against intimate partners. Bias in acquaintance and possibly intimate partner homicide rates may result in errors in the analysis. Acquaintance rates may look more like intimate partner rates than they should because of the concurrent possibilities of intimate partner homicide occurrences within the counts and an undercount of acquaintance killings with instrumental motives. In terms of total homicide rates, the effect would be primarily a heavier representation of domestic homicides than instrumental. Despite some validity problems with the SHR, however, they are the best macroanalytical data on homicide offenders available, and as Abraham Tannenbaum (1993) states, they provide a good way to look at general trends in homicide.

This study acknowledges the potential for error and additional weaknesses in the data and has taken steps listed earlier to minimize some of these problems. It is important to reiterate that the goal of this study is one of exploration. That is, the study is examining the possibility that gender equality may be useful in explaining homicide rates. Further study is needed for more sophisticated data collection and more definitive analysis.

## Data: Independent and Control Variables for the Comparative Analysis

The comparative analysis tests indicators from the three theoretical perspectives against gender-disaggregated homicide rates. The percentage of African Americans and the poverty rate, as discussed previously, are crossover variables that appear in two or all three perspectives. The percentage of African Americans has been used as a measure of heterogeneity in social disorganization and as a proxy for the subculture of violence. All discussions regarding this variable involve heterogeneity because the subculture of violence proxy is problematic. The percentage of African Americans is measured by the percentage of the population listed in the 1990 census as black. The percentage of poor is measured by the percentage of families living below the poverty line.

Other social disorganization variables include population density, the percentage of those divorced or separated (calculated by adding the total divorced and total separated), and population change. Population density is measured as the number of persons per square mile. The percentage of those divorced and separated is measured as the total persons divorced added to total persons separated divided by the total population fifteen and older—the age the census uses to determine marital status counts. The percentage of population change is figured as the percentage of increase or decrease in the population from 1980 to 1990. All of these variables were taken from the 1990 census.

In addition to the percentage of poor and percentage of African Americans, the South is used as a subculture of violence dummy variable with a score of 1 given to cities that were in Confederate states. Additional variables include age composition, measured as the percentage of the total and female populations ages 15–39, and total population size, as recorded in the 1990 census. These traditional variables have appeared frequently in homicide studies (e.g., Williams and Flewelling, 1988; Messner, 1982; Land, McCall, and Cohen, 1990).[3]

For the comparative analysis, several variables were transformed into natural logs to correct for skew. These variables were the percentage of African Americans, population density, population change, and the percentage male or female ages 15–39. Population size and poverty were not skewed over 1.

Two analytical procedures were conducted for this comparative analysis. First, ordinary least squares (OLS) regression was run with men's and women's homicide offending rates, both overall and victim-offender relationship specific, regressed on the traditional predictors. Second, seemingly unrelated regression (SURE) was run using the SAS mainframe program. Although SURE does not improve upon OLS estimates in this particular type of analysis, it allows for testing of the significance of difference between coefficients for the same variable between the models.[4] A t-test was generated from the maximum likelihood estimation technique used in the SURE analysis and was used to test for significant differences between the men's and women's homicide analyses.[5]

## Data: Independent and Control Variables
## for the Analysis of Women's Homicide Rates

The analysis of gender equality and women's homicide rates extends what is explained by traditional predictors. Measures of gender equality tap two dimensions: social and economic. The social dimension includes three indicators. (1) Unmarried household, or cohabitation, rate is calculated by the number of census-identified households composed of unmarried couples, heterosexual or homosexual, divided by the population multiplied by 100,000. (2) The percentage of women divorced or separated is computed by figuring the percentage of the total population of women fifteen and older who were divorced or separated according to the census. (3) The percentage of male single-headed households is also calculated from census figures. The number of men who singly headed households with children is figured as a percentage of the total number of single-headed households with children. High scores on these three variables indicate high levels of gender equality with regard to gender expectations involving marriage and child rearing.

The unmarried household, or cohabitation, rate reflects alternative relationship structures. For couples to be a part of this group, they had to be living together and report that they were unmarried but cohabiting in more than an acquaintance relationship. Thus cohabiting couples are engaged in somewhat stable and committed relationships that they were willing to report to the census but that were not marital ones. This measure differs from familial breakdown, discussed in social disorganization, in that it does not reflect the dissolution or absence of family but is merely a nontraditional form.

The percentage of women divorced or separated does reflect familial instability to a point, but it also reflects the degree to which women are living independent of men and unconstrained by traditional marital ties. The latter point strongly reflects the element of nontraditional social roles for women. It is also possible that given the critical point of divorce as a trigger for the escalation of men's violence against women, women's divorce or separation could serve as an aggravator. Because this measure includes the status of being divorced or separated, however, the aggravating factor may be less pronounced than a similar measure of women's rate of filing for divorce.

Finally, the percentage of male single-headed households with children addresses parity and nontraditional arrangements concerning care for children when parents are not together. The more men are awarded custody and take responsibility for primary care of children, the more the traditional expectations that these tasks are "women's work" are violated. Social equality as a whole is important to acknowledge because of its power to restrain or release women with regard to normative expectations to conform to traditional restrictions.

The social equality variables included in this study have not been used in the study of homicide rates for women. They were derived from theoretical discussion of social equality, women, and homicide, which suggests that expectations and structures of social opportunities will have an impact on women's lives. The predictors included were the best available at the city level to reflect the degree of traditional social behaviors and arrangements. These variables represent an extension of gender equality considerations to social dimensions as much as possible. Given the limited data from which to draw independent variables that encompass gender normative systems, these measurements of social equality stand as a test to see if the concept is generally useful and if we see some evidence that nontraditional partnership and men's caring for children have an effect on women's homicide offending.

The economic dimension of equality includes five indicators, all obtained from the census. (1) Women's employment rate is calculated using the number of women employed divided by women's population age sixteen and older (the census age for the working population) multiplied by 100,000. (2) The percentage of women in managerial and technical professions is figured as a percentage of women age sixteen and over who are working. (3) Gender equality in income is used as a relative equality variable. Women's income from work is divided by men's income from work; the proportion is then computed into a percentage. The higher the percentage, the greater the equality. (4) Gender equality in employment is also used as an equality variable. The women's employment rate is divided into the men's employment rate and converted into a percentage. Again, the higher the percentage, the greater the equality.

(5) The percentage of female single-headed households that are poor is also used. This is calculated by dividing the number of poor, female single-headed households with children by the total number of female-headed households with children. Rather than an absolute poverty measure as we see in the traditional predictors, this measure is a relative measurement of single mothers' poverty status. As a percentage of all women with children, the percentage of poor women with children represents the proportion of single women who do not have adequate resources compared to the total number of single mothers, poor or not. As the poverty of single mothers increases, we see fewer resources for single mothers, an indicator of economic support for women. The more women are self-sufficient, the less dependent they are likely to be. This is a negative measure of gender equality; as this measure increases, the less equal the city is. Overall, these indicators measure women's opportunities to obtain economic resources (employment rate, female single-headed households that

are poor), participation in higher-status employment (percentage of women in manufacturing and technical professions), and equality in pay and employment relative to men.

These economic indicators were derived from indicators used in both the Status of Women Index (Yllo, 1983) and the Gender Equality Index (Sugarman and Straus, 1988). The best indicators available at the city level were included. The "best" means the most illustrative and least problematic in terms of multicollinearity and missing data. This study extends the scales in two ways. First, the focus of this study is the city level, not the state level, and it explores associations between gender equality and women's homicide offending with a unit of analysis not previously seen. The drawback is that the data from which to draw are less rich than those at the state level, and it was impossible to create a single factor scale that encompassed each dimension of gender equality—social and economic—for cities.

A second extension relates to the age of the Kersti Yllo and Sugarman and Straus scales. Both scales include gender equality variables from 1980. This study examines data from 1990. No previous studies have used gender equality and 1990 data.

The analysis of gender equality is done in two stages. The first is an examination of how much improvement social and economic indicators add to the most useful traditional predictors. The second stage draws from this analysis to create the best possible explanatory model for women's homicide. These stages are conducted for women's overall, intimate partner, family, and acquaintance homicides.

The first analysis employs multiple regression to analyze a baseline model of the most significant predictors and controls determined in the generalizability analysis. Then a second equation adding the economic variables is estimated, and a third equation with traditional, economic equality, and social equality variables is estimated. A change in $R^2$ F test is computed between the traditional and economic equality models, the economic and social (complete) models, and the traditional and complete models.[6] These analyses determine whether these types of gender equality variables *as a group* can increase variance explained. At this stage of the analysis, the focus on the group is most useful because of multicollinearity.

The second analysis addresses both the inability to discuss individual effects in the first analysis and the desire to create the most parsimonious regression model for explaining each type of homicide.

Stepwise regression is used to derive the best set of variables from the complete model from the previous analysis. The effects of these variables, in addition to the control variables of population size and the percentage ages 15–39, were then estimated using women's homicide rates. This is done to create the best possible model from which we can infer the effects of individual variables, as well as explain women's homicide rates in general.

## Issues of Multicollinearity

The use of secondary, macrolevel data carries the ultimate problem of multicollinearity between independent variables. Macrolevel analysis of homicide is no exception. This study was also characterized by some degree of multicollinearity between independent variables, both traditional and gender equality. As much consideration as possible was given to addressing the problem of multicollinearity. Recall, however, that these findings are preliminary. This study was an exploratory examination of the potential value of considering gender in theoretical and empirical work involving women and homicide offending. This study is not a complete statement on the matter. Instead, caution is encouraged throughout the discussion to remember that the findings are suggestive, not absolutely definitive. Future research done on the topic is where specificity of measures and analytical techniques will be further developed.

Independent variables from both traditional and gender equality analyses showed some multicollinearity. In the presence of multicollinearity, factor analysis is often indicated (e.g., Land, McCall, and Cohen, 1990). It is worth noting that this is not the approach taken by every homicide study, and it is often difficult to reproduce the factor analysis done by advocates. The most commonly used traditional predictors were drawn for this study both because of their rigor and because of their history as indicators of traditional theory. Factor analysis was not helpful with these data.

Likewise, in examining the gender equality variables, attempts to scale those indicators revealed that although social and economic indicators were theoretically connected, they were not measures of the same factors when factor analysis was done. Thus the indicators were included separately. A process of elimination then occurred to pare down the list to the least related indicators, which are those discussed earlier. Despite efforts to eliminate problematic indicators, some multicollinearity is present in the entire group of gender equality indicators. Thus individual effects of social and economic equality in this analysis are less useful than the the overall additions as a group of variables, and conclusions should be drawn from the additional explanatory power of the group of variables. Again, this study is a preliminary look at the utility of gender-based variables for understanding women's homicide offending. Although multicollinearity inhibits the ability to make strong definitive statements about each individual indicator, sufficient evidence demonstrates that this is a fruitful direction for women's homicide offending analysis, despite weaknesses in the data.[7]

## Notes

1. Comparison of the 1990 SHR data with the 1990 UCR data revealed that 2 of the missing cities had no homicides in 1990, 12 cities reported homicides to the UCR but not to the SHR, and 9 cities had missing data for both. Several of the 12 cities that did not report to the SHR were in Florida, which had reporting problems and did not report to the SHR in 1990. The 2 cities that reported no homicides to the UCR—Scottsdale, Arizona, and Irvine, California—were recoded as zero for all categories of homicide incidences. The totals for the 12 cities that reported to the UCR were added to the city total variable. Thus 179 cities were available for gender-specific analysis, and 191 cities were used for aggregated homicide summary statistics.

Analysis was done on the 21 cities with missing SHR data to determine if there were patterns that might influence the overall analysis. Logistic regression was used to analyze independent variables on a dummy-coded measure that reflected whether homicide data were missing (1 = missing). This was done for both the traditional homicide and gender equality variables.

The traditional variable analysis included the percentage in poverty, 1990 population, percentage divorced or separated, the South, percentage male 15–39 (logged), percentage female 15–39 (logged), percentage African American (logged), population density (logged), and percentage change in population from 1980 to 1990 (logged). The chi-square for the equation was significant at <0.01, but the significance resulted from three variables: the South (positive; $p = 0.003$), percentage female 15–39 (negative; $p = 0.01$), and population density (positive; $p = 0.019$). Thus there were greater odds of missing data if the city was in the South, had fewer younger women, and had greater population density. The relationships for the South and population density may be understated, as there were more missing data for cities high on these variables. Likewise, there is a risk of overstatement of percentage female 15–39 in analyses with this variable. No other variables were significantly represented in missing data.

Analysis with gender equality variables showed no significant patterns with respect to missing data and an insignificant chi-square for the collection of variables in the logistic regression model.

2. The weighting and adjusting procedure described by Williams and Flewelling (1987) was developed to correct for two problems with SHR data. The first pertains to discrepancies in total counts between Uniform Crime Reports data and the SHR. The SHR usually contains underreports with respect to the UCR. A weight factor was calculated by dividing UCR counts by SHR counts. The SHR counts were then multiplied by this weight factor to obtain adjusted counts.

Missing data on victim-offender relationships were adjusted by using extrapolation of information from cases with complete information to cases with missing data based on a third characteristic. The formula used was

$$[a + (a_1/n_1)m_1]/P \times 100,000$$

where a refers to the number of incidents with the characteristic, $a_1$ is the number of incidents with the specific characteristic in a circumstance category, $n_1$ is the number of circumstance category i incidents with valid values on the characteristic of interest, and $m_1$ is the number of circumstance category i incidents with missing values on the characteristics of interest. This adjusted rate is based on an independent distribution for each circumstance type within the known cases. This calculation distributes the number of cases with unknown victim-offender relationships based on the percentage distribution of cases where victim-offender relationship is known. This assumes that the real distribution of the unknown cases is the same as the known cases. Although it is likely to be biased, it is a better attempt to account for the unknown cases than accepting biased data without adjustment. It cannot, however, approximate either cases that do not come to the attention of law enforcement or errors in the classification of known cases, both potential sources of bias for which compensation cannot be done.

3. These variables have been commonly used in homicide theory as indicators of social disorganization, but they are not the best reflection of the theory. The primary focus of social disorganization is on the inefficiency or complete lack of neighborhood bonds, which results in crime. These indicators do not capture this process. Additionally, some of the concepts in the theory are inadequately represented by these indicators. Heterogeneity, for example, is a much more complex concept than racial composition, which percentage African American or percentage nonwhite measures. The variables included in this analysis should be taken as established indicators

used in previous homicide studies that need to be tested against gender-disaggregated homicide rates. They should not be taken as the best possible test of social disorganization.

4. SURE is normally used to compare equations whose error terms are correlated because of mutual influence. SURE writes the individual equations as one large equation, estimates the correlated error as an unmeasured factor, and improves the overall efficiency of both equations through the control of the common, unmeasured factor(s) (Kennedy, 1996). Although women's and men's homicide rates are potentially influenced by a common factor or factors, SURE did not improve on OLS estimates in this analysis because all of the individual variables are the same for the two equations. In this case, SURE estimates will be equivalent to those of OLS (see Kennedy, 1996). SURE was done because it allows for the comparison of coefficients t-test.

5. In this t-test the question addressed is whether the coefficients can be constrained to be equal. SURE estimates multiple models simultaneously and allows for this test. The t-test was performed to examine whether the two coefficients unconstrained differed significantly from the two constrained. In other words, were they essentially the same coefficient, or did they differ? The test allows for discussion beyond simple appearances. Two coefficients may be significant in OLS regression and in the same direction, but one may still be significantly different from the other. Likewise, two coefficients, one significant in OLS regression and one not, may be essentially the same. No recent studies in criminology have used either SURE or this t-test procedure.

6. The change in $R^2$ test was computed with unadjusted $R^2$ because the computation already takes into account the number of variables in the equation. The findings, however, will report the adjusted $R^2$ because of the need to examine variance explained taking the number of variables into account.

7. The presence of multicollinearity between indicators often calls for factor analysis–based scaling, which relatively weights indicators and creates composite measures that reflect only one factor. This technique was attempted with these data. The research began with four social variables and ten economic variables in its original conception. The end result was a multifactor solution in each. The four social indicators fell into three factors, indicating that the variables were sufficiently different to include separately. Examination of the correlations among the four initial variables revealed that a measure of fertility that was used was highly correlated with the others and thus was dropped. The remaining social variables were only moderately correlated. $R^2$ analysis run regressing each on the others revealed the same general results. Although the three variables remaining did not hold together as a single factor mathematically, the previously mentioned rationale for including them makes a theoretical argument that they are all related.

As mentioned, the examination of economic indicators began with ten. In addition to the female employment rate, percentage in managerial and technical professions, percentage of single mothers with children in poverty, and the gender gaps in employment and income discussed previously, the study also considered female unemployment and two other measures of women in poverty. Factor analysis led to a four-factor solution. From these, the two most understandable—relative inequality (gender gaps in income and employment) and economic status and resources (female unemployment and employment rates, percentage in managerial and technical professions, and percentage single mothers in poverty)—were kept and tried. These factors did not work as well in the analysis as the six indicators represented did separately. This suggested that the scales created by factor analysis were covering some differences that were individually important. Multicollinearity analysis revealed moderate correlations and $R^2$ for the economic variables. The primary exception was female unemployment, which was very highly correlated. This variable was dropped.

Multicollinearity among the gender equality variables is moderate but not overwhelming ($r^2 = 0.5$ or lower; $R^2 = 0.78$ or lower). As scales have not been produced, individual coefficients in blocks cannot be given too much weight. The test of overall improvement in prediction can be addressed, however. This was the reason for the focus on the F test for change in $R^2$.

Multicollinearity is present between some of the gender equality indicators and traditional indicators. The two types of indicators that are highly correlated are those that pertain to poverty and divorce. Percentage divorced or separated and percentage of women divorced or separated are very highly correlated. Percentage of female-headed households with children that are poor and percentage of families in poverty are also highly correlated. This raises questions about overlap between traditional and gender equality models. The correlations between the two divorce variables reflect the fact that women who are divorced or separated are necessarily part of the overall number. This fact raises problems in sorting out the effects of gender equality versus the traditional factors. The poverty overlap reflects a similar process but also indicates the high representation of poor women in the overall number of families in poverty. Our poverty measures could be reflecting high numbers of single women with children who are poor, which may be the operating feature of poverty-homicide relationships. Another interpretation could be that overall poverty places women at particular risk to be poor single mothers.

The high correlations between the divorce and poverty variables cloud the distinction in these cases between traditional and gender equality predictors. This problem results largely from the crudeness of the measures and the lack of data availability. Secondary research, particularly at the macro level, is susceptible to these problems, as it is dependent on what has been collected. Thus the tests of gender equality can be construed as conservative, given the overlap between the traditional and gender equality variables. Significant findings in the face of this multicollinearity would be an even stronger indication of the influence of gender equality than would be the case otherwise because of the confounding and weakening influence provided by the overlap in the indicators.

# APPENDIX B:
# GENDER EQUALITY
# ANALYSIS TABLES

**Table B.1   Traditional Homicide Predictors and Women's Total Homicide Rates**

| Variable | b | Beta | p |
|---|---|---|---|
| Log of percentage African American | 0.179 | 0.274 | <0.001 |
| Percentage of families in poverty | 0.041 | 0.286 | <0.001 |
| Log of percentage population change | −0.297 | −0.061 | 0.370 |
| Log of population density | −0.159 | −0.132 | 0.054 |
| Percentage of total population divorced or separated | 0.082 | 0.201 | 0.003 |
| Confederate South | 0.233 | 0.121 | 0.068 |
| Percentage female 15–39 | −0.010 | −0.039 | 0.532 |
| Population size (1990) | <0.001 | 0.089 | 0.118 |
| Adjusted $R^2$ | | 0.500 | |
| Significance of F | | <0.001 | |

**Table B.2   Traditional Homicide Predictors and Women's Intimate Partner Homicide Rates**

| Variable | b | Beta | p |
|---|---|---|---|
| Log of percentage African American | 0.114 | 0.226 | 0.012 |
| Percentage of families in poverty | 0.027 | 0.247 | 0.005 |
| Log of percentage population change | 0.110 | 0.029 | 0.712 |
| Log of population density | −0.149 | −0.160 | 0.047 |
| Percentage of total population divorced or separated | 0.050 | 0.158 | 0.046 |
| Confederate South | 0.114 | 0.077 | 0.320 |
| Percentage female 15–39 | −0.029 | −0.146 | 0.039 |
| Population size (1990) | <0.001 | 0.039 | 0.556 |
| Adjusted $R^2$ | | 0.320 | |
| Significance of F | | <0.001 | |

**Table B.3    Traditional Homicide Predictors and Women's Family Homicide Rates**

| Variable | b | Beta | p |
|---|---|---|---|
| Log of percentage African American | 0.046 | 0.125 | 0.193 |
| Percentage of families in poverty | 0.013 | 0.160 | 0.085 |
| Log of percentage population change | −0.008 | −0.003 | 0.971 |
| Log of population density | −0.016 | −0.023 | 0.785 |
| Percentage of total population divorced or separated | 0.056 | 0.244 | 0.005 |
| Confederate South | 0.111 | 0.103 | 0.215 |
| Percentage female 15–39 | −0.013 | −0.090 | 0.242 |
| Population size (1990) | <0.001 | 0.068 | 0.337 |
| Adjusted $R^2$ | | 0.215 | |
| Significance of F | | <0.001 | |

**Table B.4    Traditional Homicide Predictors and Women's Acquaintance Homicide Rates**

| Variable | b | Beta | p |
|---|---|---|---|
| Log of percentage African American | 0.061 | 0.128 | 0.145 |
| Percentage of families in poverty | 0.020 | 0.191 | 0.026 |
| Log of percentage population change | −0.604 | −0.170 | 0.030 |
| Log of population density | −0.008 | −0.009 | 0.905 |
| Percentage of total population divorced or separated | 0.059 | 0.198 | 0.012 |
| Confederate South | 0.306 | 0.218 | 0.005 |
| Percentage female 15–39 | 0.021 | 0.114 | 0.110 |
| Population size (1990) | <0.001 | 0.099 | 0.130 |
| Adjusted $R^2$ | | 0.339 | |
| Significance of F | | <0.001 | |

# REFERENCES

Abbott, Pamela, and Claire Wallace. 1990. *An Introduction to Sociology: Feminist Perspectives.* New York: Routledge.

Adler, Freda. 1975. *Sisters in Crime.* New York: McGraw-Hill.

Albrecht, Stan. 1980. "Reactions and Adjustments to Divorce: Differences in the Experiences of Males and Females." *Family Relations.* 29:59–68.

Barnett, Ola, Cindy Miller-Perrin, and Robin Perrin. 1997. *Family Violence Across the Lifespan.* Thousand Oaks: Sage.

Baron, Larry. 1993. "Gender Inequality and Child Homicide: A State-Level Analysis." Pp. 207–225 in Anna Wilson (ed.), *Homicide: The Victim/Offender Connection.* Cincinnati: Anderson.

Belknap, Joanne. 1996. *The Invisible Woman: Gender, Crime, and Justice.* New York: Wadsworth.

Bernhard, Linda. 2000. "Physical and Sexual Violence Experienced by Lesbian and Heterosexual Women." *Violence Against Women.* 6:68–79.

Best, Joel, and David Luckinbill. 1990. "Male Dominance and Female Criminality: A Test of Harris's Theory of Deviant Type-Scripts." *Sociological Inquiry.* 6:71–86.

Blau, Judith, and Peter Blau. 1982. "Metropolitan Structure and Violent Crime." *American Sociological Review.* 47:114–128.

Block, Carolyn Rebecca. 1993. "Lethal Violence in the Chicago Latino Community." Pp. 267–342 in Anna Wilson (ed.), *Homicide: The Victim-Offender Connection.* Cincinnati: Anderson.

Blumstein, Philip, and Pepper Schwartz. 1991. "Money and Ideology: Their Impact on Power and Division of Household Labor." Pp. 261–288 in Rae Leiser Blumberg (ed.), *Gender, Family, and Economy: The Triple Overlap.* Thousand Oaks: Sage.

Bograd, Michele. 1988. "How Battered Women and Abusive Men Account for Domestic Violence: Excuses, Justifications, or Explanations?" In Gerald Hotaling et al. (eds.), *Coping with Family Violence: Research and Policy Perspectives.* Thousand Oaks: Sage.

Boudreau, Frances. 1993. "Elder Abuse." Pp. 142–158 in Robert Hampton et al. (eds.), *Family Violence: Prevention and Treatment*. Newbury Park: Sage.

Bowker, Lee. 1998. *Masculinities and Violence*. Thousand Oaks: Sage

———. 1993. "A Battered Woman's Problems Are Social, Not Psychological." Pp. 82–96 in Richard Gelles and Donileen Loseke (eds.), *Current Controversies in Family Violence*. Newbury Park: Sage.

Brewer, Victoria, and M. Dwayne Smith. 1995. "Gender Inequality and Rates of Female Homicide Victimization Across United States Cities." *Journal of Research in Crime and Delinquency*. 32:175–190.

Brod, Harry. 1994. "Some Thoughts on Some Histories of Some Masculinities." Pp. 82–96 in Harry Brod and Michael Kaufman (eds.), *Theorizing Masculinities*. Thousand Oaks: Sage.

Browne, Angela. 1997. "Violence in Marriage: Until Death Do Us Part?" Pp. 48–69 in A. P. Cardarelli (ed.), *Violence Between Intimate Partners: Patterns, Causes, and Effects*. Needham Heights, MA: Allyn and Bacon.

———. 1987. *When Battered Women Kill*. New York: Free Press.

Browne, Angela, and Kirk Williams. 1993. "Gender Intimacy–Lethal Violence: Trends from 1976 Through 1987." *Gender and Society*. 7:78–98.

———. 1989 "Exploring the Effect of Resource Availability and the Likelihood of Female-Perpetrated Homicides." *Law and Society Review*. 23:75–94.

Browne, Angela, Kirk Williams, and Donald Dutton. 1999. "Homicide Between Intimate Partners: A 20-Year Review." Pp. 149–164 in M. Dwayne Smith and Margaret Zahn (eds.), *Homicide: A Sourcebook of Social Research*. Thousand Oaks: Sage.

Bursik, Robert J. 1988. "Social Disorganization and Theories of Crime and Delinquency: Problems and Prospects." *Criminology*. 26:519–551.

Busch, K. G., R. Zagar, J. R. Hughes, J. Arbit et al. 1990. "Adolescents Who Kill." *Journal of Clinical Psychology*. 46:472–485.

Campbell, Anne. 1993. *Men, Women, and Aggression*. New York: Basic.

———. 1986. "The Streets and Violence." Pp. 115–132 in Anne Campbell and John Gibbs (eds.), *Violent Transactions: The Limits of Personality*. New York: Basil Blackwell.

———. 1981. *Girl Delinquents*. New York: St. Martin's.

Campbell, J. 1992. "If I Can't Have You, No One Can: Power and Control in the Homicide of Female Partners." Pp. 99–113 in J. Radford and D.E.H. Russell (eds.), *Femicide and the Politics of Women Killing*. New York: Twayne.

Cao, Liqun, Anthony Adams, and Vickie Jensen. 1997. "A Test of the Black Subculture of Violence Thesis: A Research Note." *Criminology*. 35:367–379

———. 1996. "The Black Subculture of Violence: A Test of the Popular

Thesis." Paper presented to the Academy of Criminal Justice Sciences, Las Vegas.

Carlen, Pat, and Anne Worrall. 1987. *Gender, Crime, and Justice.* Milton Keynes: Open University Press.

Carlson, Bonnie. 1987. "Wife-Battering: A Social Deviance Analysis." Pp. 172–196 in Josefina Figueira-McDonough and Rosemari Sarri (eds.), *The Trapped Woman: Catch–22 in Deviance and Control.* Newbury Park: Sage.

Cazenave, Noel, and Margaret Zahn. 1992. "Women, Murder, and Male Domination: Police Reports of Domestic Violence in Chicago and Philadelphia." Pp. 83–97 in Emilio Viano (ed.), *Intimate Violence: Interdisciplinary Perspectives.* Bristol, PA: Taylor and Francis.

Chafetz, Janet Saltzman. 1991. "The Gendered Division of Labor and the Reproduction of Female Disadvantage: Toward an Integrated Theory." Pp. 74–96 in Rae Leiser Blumberg (ed.), *Gender, Family, and Economy: The Triple Overlap.* Thousand Oaks: Sage.

Chandler, Joan. 1991. *Women Without Husbands: An Exploration of the Margins of Marriage.* New York: St. Martin's Press.

Chapple, Constance. 1998. "Dow Corning and the Silicone Breast Implant Debacle: A Case of Corporate Crime Against Women." In Lee Bowker (ed.), *Masculinities and Violence.* Thousand Oaks: Sage.

Chesney-Lind, Meda. 1989. "Girls' Crime and Woman's Place: Toward a Feminist Model of Female Delinquency." *Crime and Delinquency.* 35:5–29.

Chesney-Lind, Meda, and Randall Shelden. 1992. *Girls, Delinquency, and Juvenile Justice.* Belmont, CA: Wadsworth.

Chimbos, Peter. 1978. *Marital Violence: A Study of Interspousal Homicide.* San Francisco: R and E Research Associates.

Coggeshall, John. 1991. "Those Who Surrender Are Female: Prisoner Gender Identities as Cultural Mirror." Pp. 81–96 in Pamela Frese and John Coggeshall (eds.), *Transcending Boundaries: Multidisciplinary Approaches to the Study of Gender.* New York: Bergin and Garvey.

Collier, Richard. 1998. *Masculinities, Crime, and Criminology.* London: Sage.

Coltrane, Scott. 1994. "Theorizing Masculinities in Contemporary Social Science." Pp. 39–60 in Harry Brod and Michael Kaufman (eds.), *Theorizing Masculinities.* Thousand Oaks: Sage.

Connell, R. W. 1995. *Masculinities.* Berkeley: University of California Press.

Cook, Dee. 1987. "Women on Welfare: In Crime or Injustice?" Pp. 28–42 in Pat Carlen and Anne Worrall (eds.), *Gender, Crime, and Justice.* Milton Keynes: Open University Press.

Corzine, Jay, Lin Huff-Corzine, and Hugh Whitt. 1999. "Cultural and Subcultural Theories of Homicide." Pp. 42–57 in M. Dwayne Smith and Margaret Zahn (eds.), *Homicide: A Sourcebook of Social Research.* Thousand Oaks: Sage.

Daly, Kathleen, and Meda Chesney-Lind. 1988. "Feminism and Criminology." *Justice Quarterly.* 5:497–533.

Daly, Martin, and Margo Wilson. 1988. *Homicide.* New York: Aldine de Gruyter.

Davis, Angela. 1981. *Women, Race, and Class.* New York: Vintage.

de Beauvoir, Simone. 1953. *The Second Sex.* New York: Alfred A. Knopf.

Dennehy, Katherine, and Jeylan Mortimer. 1993. "Work and Family Orientations of Contemporary Adolescent Boys and Girls." Pp. 87–107 in Jane Hood (ed.), *Men, Work, and the Family.* Thousand Oaks: Sage.

Dunn, Dana, Elizabeth Almquist, and Janet Saltzman Chafetz. 1993. "Macrostructural Perspectives on Gender Inequality." Pp. 69–90 in Paula England (ed.), *Theory on Gender: Feminism on Theory.* New York: Aldine de Gruyter.

Dutton, Donald, and J. J. Browning. 1988. "Concern for Power, Fear of Intimacy, and Aversive Stimuli for Wife Assault." Pp. 163–175 in Gerald Hotaling et al. (eds.), *Family Abuse and Its Consequences: New Directions in Research.* Thousand Oaks: Sage.

Dutton, Donald, and Susan Golant. 1995. *The Batterer: A Psychological Profile.* New York: Basic.

Elliott, Delbert, and David Huizinga. 1983. "Social Class and Delinquent Behavior in a National Youth Panel: 1976–1980." *Criminology.* 21:149–177.

Elliott, Delbert, David Huizinga, and Suzanne Ageton. 1985. *Explaining Delinquency and Drug Use.* Beverly Hills: Sage.

Elliott, Delbert, David Huizinga, and Scott Menard. 1989. *Multiple Problem Youth: Delinquency, Substance Use, and Mental Health Problems.* New York: Springer-Verlag.

Elliott, Delbert, William Julius Wilson, David Huizinga, Robert Sampson, Amanda Elliott, and Bruce Rankin. 1996. "The Effects of Neighborhood Disadvantage on Adolescent Development." *Journal of Research in Crime and Delinquency.* 33:389–426.

England, Paula, and Irene Browne. 1992. "Trends in Women's Economic Status." *Sociological Perspectives.* 35:17–51.

Ewing, Charles Patrick. 1997. *Fatal Families: The Dynamics of Intrafamilial Homicide.* Thousand Oaks: Sage.

———. 1990. *When Children Kill: The Dynamics of Juvenile Homicide.* Lexington: Lexington Books.

Fagan, Jeffrey, Douglas Steward, and Karen Hansen. 1983. "Violent Men or Violent Husbands? Background Factors and Situational Correlates." Pp. 49–68 in David Finkelhor et al. (eds.), *The Dark Side of Families: Current Family Violence Research.* Newbury Park: Sage.

Fassinger, Polly. 1993. "Meanings of Housework for Single Fathers and Mothers: Insights into Gender Equality." Pp. 195–216 in Jane Hood (ed.), *Men, Work, and the Family.* Thousand Oaks: Sage.

Featherstone, Brid. 1996. "Victims or Villains? Women Who Physically

Abuse Their Children." Pp. 178–189 in Barbara Fawcett et al. (eds.), *Violence and Gender Relations: Theories and Interventions.* London: Sage.

Federal Bureau of Investigation. 1996. *Crime in the United States.* Washington, DC: U.S. Government Printing Office.

Feiring, Candice, and Deborah Coates. 1987. "Social Networks and Gender Differences in the Life Space of Opportunity: Introduction." *Sex Roles.* 17:611–620.

Ferraro, Kathleen. 1997. "Battered Women: Strategies for Survival." Pp. 124–140 in Albert P. Cardarelli (ed.), *Violence Between Intimate Partners: Patterns, Causes, and Effects.* Boston: Allyn and Bacon.

———. 1988. "An Existential Approach to Battering." Pp. 126–138 in Gerald Hotaling et al. (eds.), *Family Abuse and Its Consequences: New Directions in Research.* Thousand Oaks: Sage.

Finkelhor, David, and Karl Pillemer. 1988. "Elder Abuse: Its Relationship to Other Forms of Domestic Violence." Pp. 244–254 in Gerald Hotaling et al. (eds.), *Family Abuse and Its Consequences: New Directions in Research.* Thousand Oaks: Sage.

Fox, Greer Litton, and Jan Allen. 1987. "Child Care." in Josefina Figueira-McDonough and Rosemary Sarri (eds.), *The Trapped Woman: Catch-22 in Deviance and Control.* Newbury Park: Sage.

Fraad, Harriet, Stephen Resnick, and Richard Wolff. 1994. *Bringing It All Back Home: Class, Gender, and Power in the Modern Household.* Boulder: Pluto.

Gartner, Rosemary, Kathryn Baker, and Fred Pampel. 1990. "Gender Stratification and the Gender Gap in Homicide Victimization." *Social Problems.* 37:593–612.

Gelles, Richard. 1997. *Intimate Violence in Families,* 3d ed. Thousand Oaks: Sage.

———. 1993. "Through a Sociological Lens: Social Structure and Family Violence." Pp. 31–46 in Richard Gelles and Donileen Loseke (eds.), *Current Controversies on Family Violence.* Newbury Park: Sage.

Gillespie, Cynthia. 1989. *Justifiable Homicide: Battered Women, Self-Defense, and the Law.* Columbus: Ohio State University Press.

Goetting, Ann. 1990. "Child Victims of Homicide: A Portrait of the Killers and the Circumstances of Their Deaths." *Violence and Victims.* 5:287–296.

———. 1988. "Patterns of Homicide Among Women." *Journal of Interpersonal Violence.* 3:3–20.

———. 1987. "Homicidal Wives: A Profile." *Journal of Family Issues.* 8:332–341.

Gold, M. 1970. *Delinquent Behavior in an American City.* Belmont: Brooks-Cole.

Gold, M., and D. J. Reimer. 1975. "Changing Patterns of Delinquent

Behavior Among Americans 13–16 Years Old: 1967–1972." *Crime and Delinquency Literature.* 7:483–517.

Gondolf, Edward. 1993. "Male Batterers." Pp. 230–257 in Robert Hampton et. al. (eds.), *Family Violence: Prevention and Treatment.* Newbury Park: Sage.

Greenblat, Cathy Stein. 1983. "A Hit Is a Hit Is a Hit or Is It? Approval and Tolerance of Physical Force by Spouses." Pp. 235–260 in David Finkelhor et al. (eds.), *The Dark Side of Families: Current Family Violence Research.* Thousand Oaks: Sage.

Hagedorn, John. 1998. "Frat Boys, Bossmen, Studs, and Gentlemen: A Typology of Gang Masculinities." Pp. 152–167 in Lee Bowker (ed.), *Masculinities and Violence.* Thousand Oaks: Sage.

Hampton, Robert L., and Alice F. Washington Coner-Edwards. 1993. "Physical and Sexual Violence in Marriage." Pp. 113–141 in Robert Hampton et al. (eds.), *Family Violence: Prevention and Treatment.* Newbury Park: Sage.

Harris, Adrienne, and Ynestra King. 1989. *Rocking the Ship of State: Toward a Feminist Peace Politics.* Boulder: Westview.

Hearn, Jeff. 1998. *The Violences of Men.* London: Sage.

Hearn, Jeff, and David Collinson. 1994. "Theorizing Unities and Differences Between Men and Between Masculinities." Pp. 97–118 in Harry Brod and Michael Kaufman (eds.), *Theorizing Masculinites.* Thousand Oaks: Sage.

Heide, Kathleen. 1999. "Youth Homicide: An Integration of Psychological, Sociological, and Biological Approaches." Pp. 221–238 in M. Dwayne Smith and Margaret Zahn (eds.), *Homicide: A Sourcebook of Social Research.* Thousand Oaks: Sage.

———. 1992. *Why Kids Kill Parents: Child Abuse and Adolescent Homicide.* Columbus: Ohio State University Press.

Hill, Gary, and Anthony Harris. 1981. "Changes in the Gender Patterning of Crime, 1953–1977: Opportunity Versus Identity." *Social Science Quarterly.* 67:658–671.

Hill-Collins, Patricia. 1991. *Black Feminist Thought: Knowledge, Consciousness, and the Politics of Empowerment.* New York: Routledge.

Hochschild, Arlie. 1989 *The Second Shift: Working Parents and the Revolution at Home.* New York: Viking Penguin.

Holmes, Ronald, and Stephen Holmes. 1994. *Murder in America.* Thousand Oaks: Sage.

Hondagneu-Sotelo, Pierrette, and Michael Messner. 1994. "Gender Displays and Men's Power: The 'New Man' and the Mexican Immigrant Man." Pp. 200–218 in Harry Brod and Michael Kaufman (eds.), *Theorizing Masculinities.* Thousand Oaks: Sage.

Hood, Jane (ed.). 1993. *Men, Work, and the Family.* Thousand Oaks: Sage.

hooks, bell. 1984. *Feminist Theory: From Margin to Center.* Boston: South End.

Hooyman, Nancy, and Rosemary Ryan. 1987. "Women as Caregivers of the Elderly: Catch–22 Dilemmas." Pp. 143–171 in Josefina Figueria-McDonough and Rosemary Sarri (eds.), *The Trapped Woman: Catch–22 in Deviance and Control.* Newbury Park: Sage.

Isaac, Walter. 1999. "Integrating Love and Power: Reflections on Power, Helplessness, Nurture, and Men's Identity." Pp. 55–76 in Joseph Kuypers (ed.), *Men and Power.* New York: Prometheus.

Jack, Dana Crowley. 1999. *Behind the Mask: Destruction and Creativity in Women's Aggression.* Cambridge: Harvard University Press.

Jankowski, Martin Sanchez. 1991. *Islands in the Street: Gangs and American Urban Society.* Berkeley: University of California Press.

Jensen, Vickie. 1990. Fieldnotes from Mabel Bassett Correctional Center, Oklahoma City, OK.

Johnson, Miriam. 1988. *Strong Mothers, Weak Wives.* Berkeley: University of California Press.

Jurik, Nancy, and Peter Gregware. 1992. "A Method for Murder: The Study of Homicides by Women." *Perspectives on Social Problems.* 4:179–201.

Jurik, Nancy, and Russ Winn. 1990. "Gender and Homicide: A Comparison of Men and Women Who Kill." *Violence and Victims.* 5:227–242.

Kelly, Liz. 1996. "When Does the Speaking Profit Us? Reflections on the Challenges of Developing Feminist Perspectives on Abuse and Violence by Women." Pp. 34–49 in Marianne Hester, Liz Kelly, and Jill Radford (eds.), *Women, Violence, and Male Power.* Philadelphia: Open University Press.

Kennedy, Peter. 1996. *A Guide to Econometrics,* 3d ed. Cambridge: MIT Press.

Kimmel, Michael. 1996. *Manhood in America: A Cultural History.* New York: Free Press.

———. 1994. "Masculinity as Homophobia: Fear, Shame, and Silence in the Construction of Gender Identity." Pp. 119–141 in Harry Brod and Michael Kaufman (eds.), *Theorizing Masculinities.* Thousand Oaks: Sage.

Klein, Dorie. 1995. "Crime Through Gender's Prism: Feminist Criminology in the United States." Pp. 216–240 in Nicole Hahn Rafter and Frances Heidensohn (eds.), *International Feminist Perspectives in Criminology: Engendering a Discipline.* Philadelphia: Open University Press.

Kornhauser, Ruth. 1978. *Social Sources of Delinquency.* Chicago: University of Chicago Press.

Krohn, Marvin, Susan Stern, Terence Thornberry, and Sung Joon Jang. 1992. "The Measurement of Family Process Variables: The Effect of Adolescent and Parent Perceptions of Family Life on Delinquent Behavior." *Journal of Quantitative Criminology.* 8:287–315.

Kurz, Demie. 1989. "Social Science Perspectives on Wife Abuse: Current Debates and Future Directions." *Gender and Society.* 3:489–505.

———. 1999 "The Paradox of Men's Power." Pp. 17–36 in Joseph Kuypers (ed.), *Men and Power.* Amherst, NY: Prometheus.

Land, Kenneth, Patricia McCall, and Lawrence Cohen. 1990. "Structural Covariates of Homicide Rates: Are There Any Invariates Across Time and Social Space?" *American Journal of Sociology.* 95:922–963.

Langan, Patrick, and John Dawson. 1995. *Spouse Murder Defendants in Large Urban Counties.* Washington, DC: U.S. Department of Justice, Bureau of Justice Statistics. NCJ 153256.

Levant, Ronald, and Gini Kopecky. 1995. *Masculinity Reconsidered: Changing the Rules of Manhood at Work, in Relationships, and in Family Life.* New York: Penguin.

Loftin, Colin, and Robert Hill. 1974. "Regional Subculture and Homicide: An Examination of the Gastil-Hackney Thesis." *American Sociological Review.* 39:714–724.

Mac An Ghaill, Mairtin. 1994. "The Making of Black English Masculinities." Pp. 183–199 in Harry Brod and Michael Kaufman (eds.), *Theorizing Masculinities.* Thousand Oaks: Sage.

MacKinnon, Catharine A. 1987. *Feminism Unmodified: Discourses on Life and Law.* Cambridge: Harvard University Press.

Mahoney, Martha. 1994. "Victimization or Oppression? Women's Lives, Violence and Agency." Pp. 59–92 in Martha Fineman and Roxanne Mykitiuk (eds.), *The Public Nature of Private Violence: The Discovery of Domestic Abuse.* New York: Routledge.

Mann, Coramae Richey. 1996. *Women Who Kill.* Albany: State University of New York Press.

———. 1993. "Maternal Filicide of Preschoolers." Pp. 227–246 in Anna Wilson (ed.), *Homicide: The Victim/Offender Connection.* Cincinnati: Anderson.

———. 1992. "Female Murderers and Their Motives: A Tale of Two Cities." Pp. 73–81 in Emilio Viano (ed.), *Intimate Violence: Interdisciplinary Perspectives.* Bristol, PA: Taylor and Francis.

———. 1988. "Getting Even? Women Who Kill in Domestic Encounters." *Justice Quarterly.* 5:333–351.

———. 1984. *Female Crime and Delinquency.* Tuscaloosa: University of Alabama Press.

Margolin, Leslie. 1992. "Beyond Maternal Blame: Physical Child Abuse as a Phenomenon of Gender." *Journal of Family Issues.* 13:410–423.

Maxfield, Michael. 1989. "Circumstances in Supplementary Homicide Reports: Variety and Validity." *Criminology.* 27:671–695.

Messerschmidt, James. 1995. "From Patriarchy to Gender: Feminist Theory, Criminology, and the Challenge of Diversity." Pp. 167–188 in Nicole Hahn Rafter and Frances Heidensohn (eds.), *International Feminist*

*Perspectives in Criminology: Engendering a Discipline.* Philadelphia: Open University Press.

———. 1993. *Masculinities and Crime: Critique and Reconceptualization of Theory.* Lanham, MD: Rowman and Littlefield.

———. 1986. *Capitalism, Patriarchy, and Crime: Toward a Socialist-Feminist Criminology.* Totowa, NJ: Rowman and Littlefield.

Messner, Steven. 1982. "Poverty, Inequality, and the Urban Homicide Rate." *Criminology.* 20:103–114.

Messner, Steven, and Richard Rosenfeld. 1999. "Social Structure and Homicide: Theory and Research." Pp. 27–41 in M. Dwayne Smith and Margaret Zahn (eds.), *Homicide: A Sourcebook of Social Research.* Thousand Oaks: Sage.

Miller, Stuart. 1985. "Men and Friendship." In Alice Sargent (ed.), *Beyond Sex Roles.* New York: West.

Milner, Joel, and Julie Crouch. 1993. "Physical Child Abuse." Pp. 25–55 in Robert L. Hampton et al. (eds.), *Family Violence: Prevention and Treatment.* Newbury Park: Sage.

Morgan, David. 1992. *Discovering Men.* London: Routledge.

Morris, Allison. 1987. *Women, Crime, and Criminal Justice.* New York: Basil Blackwell.

Mossman, Mary Jane. 1994. "Gender Equality, Family Law and Access to Justice." *International Journal of Law and the Family.* 8:357–373.

Muehlenhard, Charlene, and Melaney Linton. 1987. "Date Rape and Sexual Aggression in Dating Situations: Incidence and Risk Factors." *Journal of Counseling Psychology.* 34:186–196.

National Research Council. 1993. *Understanding Child Abuse and Neglect.* Washington, DC: National Academy Press.

Neapolitan, Jerome. 1998. "Cross-National Variation in Homicides: Is Race a Factor?" *Criminology.* 36:139–156.

Newburn, Tim, and Elizabeth Stanko (eds.). 1994. *Just Boys Doing Business? Men, Masculinities, and Crime.* London: Routledge.

Nielson, Joyce McCarl, Russell Endo, and Barbara Ellington. 1992. "Social Isolation and Wife Abuse: A Research Report." Pp. 49–60 in Emilio Viano (ed.), *Intimate Violence: Interdisciplinary Perspectives.* Bristol, PA: Taylor and Francis.

Ogle, Robbin, Daniel Maier-Katkin, and Thomas J. Bernard. 1995. "A Theory of Homicidal Behavior Among Women." *Criminology.* 33:173–193.

Pagelow, Mildred Daly. 1981a. "Sex Roles, Power, and Woman Battering." Pp. 239–276 in Lee Bowker (ed.), *Women and Crime in America.* New York: Macmillan.

———. 1981b. "Secondary Battering and Alternatives of Female Victims to Spouse Abuse." Pp. 277–299 in Lee Bowker (ed.), *Women and Crime in America.* New York: Macmillan.

Parker, Robert Nash. 1989. "Poverty, Subculture of Violence, and Type of Homicide." *Social Forces.* 67:983–1007.

Parker, Robert Nash, and Allison Toth. 1990. "Family, Intimacy, and Homicide: A Macro-Social Approach." *Violence and Victims.* 5:195–210.

Phillips, Julie. 1997. "Variation in African-American Homicide Rates: An Assessment of Potential Explanations." *Criminology.* 35:527–559.

Polk, Kenneth. 1994a. "Masculinity, Honour, and Confrontational Homicide." Pp. 166–188 in Tim Newburn and Elizabeth Stanko (eds.), *Just Boys Doing Business? Men, Masculinities, and Crime.* London: Routledge.

———. 1994b. *When Men Kill.* Cambridge: Cambridge University Press.

Pringle, Keith. 1995. *Men, Masculinities and Social Welfare.* London: UCL Press.

Ptacek, James. 1988. "The Clinical Literature of Men Who Batter: A Review and Critique." Pp. 149–162 in Gerald Hotaling et al. (eds.), *Family Abuse and Its Consequences: New Directions in Research.* Thousand Oaks: Sage.

Ramazanoglu, Caroline. 1989. *Feminism and the Contradictions of Oppression.* New York: Routledge.

Rapaport, Karen, and Barry Burkhart. 1984. "Personality and Attitudinal Characteristics of Sexually Coercive College Males." *Journal of Abnormal Psychology.* 93:216–221.

Renzetti, Claire. 1998. "Violence and Abuse in Lesbian Relationships: Theoretical and Empirical Issues." Pp. 117–128 in Raquel Kennedy Bergen (ed.), *Issues in Intimate Violence.* Thousand Oaks: Sage.

———. 1997. "Violence and Abuse Among Same Sex Couples." Pp. 70–89 in Albert Cardarelli (ed.), *Violence Between Intimate Partners: Patterns, Causes, and Effects.* Boston: Allyn and Bacon.

Rubin, Lillian. 1994. *Families on the Fault Line.* New York: HarperCollins.

———. 1992. *Worlds of Pain: Life in the Working Class Family.* New York: Basic.

Russell, Donald. 1985. "Girls Who Kill." *International Journal of Offender Therapy and Comparative Criminology.* 29:171–176.

Saunders, Daniel. 1992. "A Typology of Men Who Batter: Three Types Derived from Cluster Analysis." *American Journal of Orthopsychiatry.* 62:264–275.

———. 1986. "When Battered Women Use Violence: Husband-Abuse or Self-Defense?" *Violence and Victims.* 1:47–60.

Schur, Edwin. 1984. *Labeling Women Deviant: Gender, Stigma, and Social Control.* New York: Random House.

Shaw, Clifford, and Henry McKay. 1972. *Juvenile Delinquency and Urban Areas.* Chicago: University of Chicago Press.

Sidel, Ruth. 1996. *Keeping Women and Children Last: America's War on the Poor.* New York: Penguin.

———. 1992. *Women and Children Last: The Plight of Poor Women in Affluent America* (rev. ed.). New York: Penguin.

Silverman, Ira, Manuel Vega, and Terry Danner. 1993. "The Female Murderer." Pp. 175–190 in Anna Wilson (ed.), *Homicide: The Victim/Offender Connection.* Cincinnati: Anderson.

Silverman, Robert, and Leslie Kennedy. 1988. "Women Who Kill Their Children." *Violence and Victims.* 3:113–127.

Simon, Rita. 1975. *Women and Crime.* Lexington, MA: Lexington Books.

Simon, Rita, and Jean Landis. 1991. *The Crimes Women Commit, the Punishments They Receive.* Lexington, MA: Lexington Books.

Simpson, Sally. 1991. "Caste, Class, and Violent Crime: Explaining Difference in Female Offending." *Criminology.* 29:115–135.

———. 1989. "Feminist Theory, Crime, and Justice." *Criminology.* 27:605–632.

Smith, Carolyn, and Terence Thornberry. 1995. "The Relationship Between Childhood Maltreatment and Adolescent Involvement in Delinquency." *Criminology.* 33:451–481.

Smith, M. Dwayne, and Victoria Brewer. 1995. "Female Status and the 'Gender Gap' in U.S. Homicide Victimization." *Violence Against Women.* 1:339–350.

———. 1992. "A Sex-Specific Analysis of Correlates of Homicide Victimization in U.S. Cities." *Violence and Victims.* 7:279–286.

Smith, Michael. 1990. "Patriarchal Ideology and Wife Beating: A Test of a Feminist Hypothesis." *Violence and Victims.* 5:257–273.

Smith-Lovin, Lynn, and J. Miller McPherson. 1993. "You Are Who You Know: A Network Approach to Gender." Pp. 223–254 in Paula England (ed.), *Theory on Gender: Feminism on Theory.* New York: Aldine de Gruyter.

Steffensmeier, Darrell. 1993. "National Trends in Female Arrests 1960–1990: Assessment and Recommendations for Research." *Journal of Quantitative Criminology.* 9:411–441.

Steffensmeier, Darrell, and Emilie Allen. 1996. "Gender and Crime: Toward a Gendered Theory of Offending." *Annual Review of Sociology.* 22:459–487.

Steffensmeier, Darrell, and Dana Haynie. 2000. "Gender, Structural Disadvantage, and Urban Crime: Do Macrosocial Variables also Explain Female Offending Rates?" *Criminology.* 38:403–438.

Steinmetz, Suzanne. 1993. "The Abused Elderly Are Dependent: Abuse Is Caused by the Perception of Stress Associated with Providing Care." Pp. 222–236 in Richard Gelles and Donileen Loseke (eds.), *Current Controversies in Family Violence.* Newbury Park: Sage.

Stoltenburg, John. 1999. "How Power Makes Men: The Grammar of Gender

Identity." Pp. 37–54 in Joseph Kuypers (ed.), *Men and Power.* New York: Prometheus.

Stout, Karen. 1991. "Women Who Kill: Offenders or Defenders?" *Affilia.* 6:8–22.

Sugarman, David, and Murray Straus. 1988. "Indicators of Gender Equality for American States and Regions." *Social Indicators Research.* 20: 229–270.

Tannenbaum, Abraham. 1993. "The Supplementary Homicide Report: A Neglected but Valuable Source for Homicide Research." Questions and Answers in Lethal and Non-Lethal Violence: Proceedings of the Second Annual Workshop of the Homicide Research Working Group. NIJ Publication 147480. Washington, DC: National Institute of Justice.

Taylor, Karen. 1991. "Patriarchy and Male Oppression: Suffering the Responsibility of Manhood." Pp. 55–66 in Pamela Frese and John Coggeshall (eds.), *Transcending Boundaries: Multidisciplinary Approaches to the Study of Gender.* New York: Bergin and Garvey.

Thornberry, Terence, Alan Lizotte, Marvin Krohn, Margaret Farnworth, and Sung Joon Jang. 1994. "Delinquent Peers, Beliefs, and Delinquent Behavior: A Longitudinal Test of Interactional Theory." *Criminology.* 32:47–83.

Totman, Jane. 1978. *The Murderess: A Psychosocial Study of Criminal Homicide.* San Francisco: R and E Research Associates.

Unnithan, N. Prabha, Lin Huff-Corzine, Jay Corzine, and Hugh Whitt. 1994. *The Currents of Lethal Violence: An Integrated Model of Suicide and Homicide.* Albany: State University of New York Press.

U.S. Bureau of the Census. 1995. "Current Population Reports, Series P29–189." Population Profile of the United States: 1995. Washington, DC: U.S. Government Printing Office.

Viano, Emilio. 1992. "Violence Among Intimates: Major Issues and Approaches." Pp. 3–12 in Emilio Viano (ed.), *Intimate Violence: Interdisciplinary Perspectives.* Bristol, PA: Taylor and Francis.

Visher, Christy. 1983. "Gender, Police Arrest Decisions, and Notions of Chivalry." *Criminology.* 21:5–28.

Walker, Lenore. 1993. "The Battered Women Syndrome Is a Psychological Consequence of Abuse." Pp. 133–153 in Richard Gelles and Donileen Loseke (eds.), *Current Controversies in Family Violence.* Newbury Park: Sage.

———. 1989. *Terrifying Love: Why Battered Women Kill and How Society Responds.* New York: HarperCollins.

Ward, David A., Maurice Jackson, and Renee Ward. 1979. "Crimes of Violence by Women." Pp. 114–138 in Freda Adler and Rita Simon (eds.), *The Criminology of Deviant Women.* Boston: Houghton Mifflin.

Websdale, Neil. 1999. *Understanding Domestic Homicide.* Boston: Northeastern University Press.

Weisheit, Ralph. 1993. "Structural Correlates of Female Homicide

Patterns." Pp. 191–206 in Anna Wilson (ed.), *Homicide: The Victim/Offender Connection*. Cincinnati: Anderson.

———. 1986. "When Mothers Kill Their Children." *Social Science Journal.* 23:439–448.

Weitzman, Lenore. 1985. *The Divorce Revolution: The Unexpected Social and Economic Consequences for Women and Children in America*. New York: Free Press.

Wilbanks, William. 1983. "Female Homicide Offenders in the U.S." *International Journal of Women's Studies.* 6:302–310.

Williams, Christine. 1995. *Still a Man's World: Men Who Do Women's Work.* Berkeley: University of California Press.

Williams, Kirk. 1984. "Economic Sources of Homicide: Reestimating the Effects of Poverty and Inequality." *American Sociological Review.* 49:283–289.

Williams, Kirk, and Robert Flewelling. 1988. "The Social Production of Criminal Homicide: A Comparative Study of Disaggregated Rates in American Cities." *American Sociological Review.* 53:421–431.

———. 1987. "Family, Acquaintance, and Stranger Homicide: Alternative Procedures for Rate Calculations." *Criminology.* 25:543–560.

Wolf, Clark. 1999. "Power and Equality in Intimate Relationships." Pp. 159–182 in Joseph Kuypers (ed.), *Men and Power*. New York: Prometheus.

Wolfgang, Marvin, and Franco Ferracuti. 1967. *The Subculture of Violence: Toward an Integrated Theory of Criminology*. London: Tavistock.

Yllo, Kersti. 1993. "Through a Feminist Lens: Gender, Power, and Violence." Pp. 47–66 in Richard Gelles and Donileen Loseke (eds.), *Current Controversies on Family Violence*. Newbury Park: Sage.

———. 1983. "Using a Feminist Approach in Quantitative Research." Pp. 277–288 in David Finkelhor et al. (eds.), *The Dark Side of Families*. Newbury Park: Sage.

Zahn, Margaret, and Patricia L. McCall. 1999. "Trends and Patterns of Homicide in the Twentieth-Century United States." Pp. 9–23 in M. Dwayne Smith and Margaret Zahn (eds.), *Homicide: A Sourcebook of Social Research*. Thousand Oaks: Sage.

# INDEX

# ABOUT THE BOOK

Traditional homicide indicators are based on male violence—and do little to predict when, or whom, women will kill. Vickie Jensen shows that gender equality plays an important role in predicting women's homicide patterns.

Jensen's analysis of the occurrence of women's homicide reveals that lethal violence is most likely when severe gender inequalities exist. Her conclusions establish the clear relationship between political, economic, legal, and social equality for women and the reduction of all forms of lethal violence.

**Vickie Jensen** is assistant professor of sociology at California State University, Northridge.